IN SEARCH OF CONFEDERATE ANCESTORS

CONFEDERATE MONUMENT, JEFFERSON, TEXAS, 1907
From Historic Southern Monuments

IN SEARCH OF CONFEDERATE ANCESTORS: THE GUIDE

BY
J. H. SEGARS

With an introduction by John McGlone

Journal of Confederate History Series
VOL. IX
Southern Heritage Press
4035 Emerald Drive
Murfreesboro, TN 37130
(615) 895-5642

Dr. John McGlone, *Editor/Publisher*

First Printing 1993
Second Printing 1993
Third Printing 1994
Fourth Printing 1996

Library of Congress Cataloging-in-Publication Data

Segars, J. H.
In Search of Confederate Ancestors
introduction by John McGlone
Includes bibliographical references and index
ISBN   0-9631963-4-0

93-16465

CIP

CONTENTS

DEDICATION

An old, dusty volume, entitled *Camp Fires of the Confederacy*, features an exquisite dedication on its frontispiece. These forgotten words, first published in 1898, best describe the intent of this guide. And may they hold true for us as we endeavor to search for our lost ancestors of the old Confederacy.

TO THE DESCENDANTS

of that brave and intrepid host who, from the beginning to the end of the long and gallant struggle of the South for political emancipation and autonomy, followed, with unwavering fortitude and devotion, its flag, and shed their blood in defense of home and kindred, these pages are dedicated, with a firm conviction that the descendants of such immortal heroes will continue to keep alive the memories, and honor the deeds, of their brave sires.

WHY SEARCH FOR CONFEDERATE ANCESTORS?

*It is to the eternal glory of the American nation
that the more hopeless became their cause, the
more desperately the Southerners fought.*
                                        –Winston Churchill

SOUTHERNERS HAVE LONG BEEN PROUD OF THEIR
heritage, and for good reason. The first English-speaking settlement
in what is now the United States was established at Jamestown in
1607. From that small outpost in Virginia, southern civilization
spread both west and south. In colonial times, aristocratic planters
from the Caribbean settled "Charles Towne," while Gov. James
Oglethorpe founded Georgia as a buffer against Spanish Florida. By
the time of the first American Revolution, the South was sufficiently
developed, to contribute to the cause of independence the fiery
Patrick Henry, the learned Thomas Jefferson, and the noble George
Washington. It is difficult to imagine American history without
these and other patriotic southerners.

With American Independence won, southerners contributed
largely to the establishment of the new government and early
leadership of the United States. It was primarily southerners who
stood with Gen. Andrew Jackson and faced and defeated the best the
British Army had to offer at New Orleans in the War of 1812. Some
of the sons and grandsons of those heroes died at the Alamo in Texas,
while others stormed the "Halls of Montezuma" in the Mexican War.
Along the way, the South seemed to be developing a soul of its own, a
peculiarly southern civilization. Southerners were Scotch-Irish,
English, French Huguenots, Acadians (Cajuns), and Africans.
Although of diverse origins, southerners would eventually share one
common, terrible ordeal, which would bind them together, the
American "Civil War."

The quotations around "Civil War" are used advisedly here. The
events of the 1860s so divided the nation, or the two nations, that to
this day historians cannot agree on what to call it. Popularly and
simplistically, it has been termed a civil war as if it were a minor
insurrection for the control of one government. It was not. To many, it
was an effort by southerners to establish (or reestablish) government
true to the original concepts of the Constitution. Hence, the southern
preference (insistence!) on calling it a War for Southern Independence
or War Between the States. From a southern perspective, the North
was changing by becoming industrialized and urbanized; in effect,
"rebelling" against the old agrarian, Jeffersonian notion of the

Founding Fathers. Accordingly, Confederates were patriots in the tradition of George Washington, Davy Crockett, and Andrew Jackson, and, like other American heroes, are deserving of our honor. If you are fortunate enough to know that you have Confederate ancestors, then you would do well to learn more about them. The following work will assist you in beginning that fascinating and invigorating search.

Southerners do not celebrate the act of war. The South has suffered a disproportionately high share of casualties in all of America's wars, including the one of 1861-65. People who have borne the battle, and their widows and orphans, do not find joy in the maimed and the dead. But what southerners do honor is courage and consistency, fortitude in the face of overwhelming odds, and devotion to "duty," a word which Gen. Robert E. Lee proclaimed to be the most sublime in the English language. Your Confederate ancestors are worthy of honor. Study them well. It would be difficult to find better models for your own conduct.

You will also take courage from their example. As you learn more about your Confederate heritage and the part your ancestor played in the cataclysmic events of the 1860s, you will discover that few people in history struggled more fiercely for their homes and their perception of the right than the Confederates. In other 19th-century warfare, Napoleon's Old Guard at Waterloo collapsed after suffering from 15 to 20 percent casualties. In the famed charge of the Light Brigade at Balaklava, made famous by Alfred Lord Tennyson, that immortal unit lost approximately one-third of its men. Yet Confederate units suffered far heavier casualties and still kept fighting. In battle after battle, Confederate ranks were decimated by losses from 40 to 60 percent and more. For example, the 1st Texas Infantry lost 82.5 percent of its men in one day at Sharpsburg. The University Grays of the 11th Mississippi were wiped out at Gettysburg, as were certain color companies of the 26th North Carolina. In 1861, the 14th Tennessee Infantry left Clarksville with 960 men. On the first day of fighting at Gettysburg two years later, the regiment numbered only 360. By the third day of the same battle, the unit entered Pickett's charge with sixty men and came out of it with two survivors. Why should we not be fascinated by ancestors who possessed such courage? That same courage was displayed on the homefront, where southern women managed plantations and farms, manufactured supplies, served as nurses and spies, and, in the words of Stephen Vincent Benèt, "Made courage from terror and bread from bran, and propped the South on a Swansdown Fan."

Should you require further evidence, consider the words of the noted historian, Bell I. Wiley, who explains why we should honor our Confederate heritage:

> There are many reasons but none is more compelling than of recognizing and honoring the greatness shown by our people during the terrible ordeal. (Southerners) justified the faith which Thomas Jefferson professed in them and their kind nearly 100 years before. Indeed, they revealed a sturdiness and a strength which probably exceeded anything envisioned by the 'sage of Monticello.' The greatness displayed by our forefathers a century ago is indeed a precious heritage, for it enables us to look forward with calm confidence to the crises which confront us and our children. Because our forefathers endured, we know that we can endure. Their strength is our strength and their example should be our standard.

Today, it is not fashionable or "politically correct" to fly Confederate battleflags, play "Dixie," or otherwise celebrate the Confederate heritage. This attitude is surely a perversion or misinterpretion of history. The history of the war was written by the victors and has been carried on in the twentieth century by a misguided press and the oversimplifications of the popular mind. Slavery has often been cited as *the* cause of the war and Abraham Lincoln as the "Great Emancipator." In that scenario, it is a simple case of right versus wrong. But the truth is far more complex. The war was fought for various social, political, and cultural reasons. Slavery was certainly an economic consideration. Yet when Confederates went to battle in 1861, they did so primarily in defense of hearth and home from an invader, while northerners did so mostly for their perceptions of preserving the Union. Today, most southerners deplore the actions of racially-motivated hate groups——North or South. But the misuse of Confederate flags or symbols by the ignorant few should not deny a whole people the right to honor their heritage. You have a right be proud of your ancestry as much as any other racial, ethnic, or national group. Your ancestors fought the good fight, served their country well, and deserve to be remembered.

On April 26, 1991, Confederate Memorial Day, Dr. Edward C. Smith of American University gave the keynote address at Arlington National Cemetery. It was an outstanding speech given by an extraordinary man. Standing before Arlington's Confederate Memorial, this distinguished black professor addressed Civil War history with truth, forthrightness, and clarity. Smith observed quite correctly that the actions and motivations of the people of the past must be judged in the context of their times, not by our own standards. He argued that the Civil War was not a contest between "Good" (the North) and "Evil" (the South), but rather a complex territorial and cultural war fought over the issue of southern independence. Pointing to a figure depicting a black soldier-in-arms in the frieze of the monument, Smith explained how some black men chose to serve in southern armies, so that they, too, might defend the only home they had ever known, and to dispel any doubts about their manhood. He eloquently stated that all participants of this most ghastly-of-all American wars deserve our understanding and respect.

The Confederate experience remains the central event of southern history. What went before was prologue and what followed is epilogue. Early Virginians emulated the "cavalier" faction of the English Civil War, while George Washington was a role model for Robert E. Lee, who has been a model for southerners ever since. Yet the focal point somehow always reverts to "The War." It was a dividing point in American history, a watershed of titantic proportions. This country was one thing before it and quite another after it, and not always for the better. But no matter how one perceives the struggle, it remains an undeniable fact that the Confederate nation taught the world the meaning of courage.

Good luck as your search for your ancestor's part in that great drama!

Murfreesboro, Tennessee   John McGlone
                                                                    Editor
                                           Journal of Confederate History

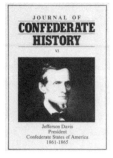

In Remembrance of
Pvt. Francis Jack Segars
16th Georgia Battalion, John C. Vaughn's Brigade

Captured: Oct. 28, 1864, at Morristown, Tennessee
Died: Dec. 8, 1864, at Camp Douglas, Illinois

His Place of Burial was Unknown
to His Family for Over a Century

-1-

★ HOW TO BEGIN ★

[The South is a place where] the past is not dead,
it isn't even past.
                                                    -William Faulkner

ANCESTRAL RESEARCHERS AND GENEALOGISTS ARE DETECTIVES. With notebooks in hand, they ask questions, conduct interviews, read archival documents, check records, visit cemeteries, and record pertinent findings. These modern detectives are on the trail of real people who lived in the past, and they have learned the secrets of how to conduct successful research.

Genealogists often refer to their work as "fitting together pieces of a giant jigsaw puzzle." While this might be a good analogy, it should go even further. Before a puzzle is put together, the individual pieces must be properly located and identified. The following are some practical tips for getting started in putting the pieces together:

- Study "how to" books on genealogy.

- Visit the local library and become familiar with its
  genealogical and Confederate collections.

- Visit or (better yet) join a   historical society; talk with
  members about their collections and activities.

- Study the history of your ancestral state and county,
  particularly from 1860 to 1865.

- Read books which are of great interest to you on the period.

- Learn how to operate a microfilm viewer at your local
  library.

- Write your state archives and request information on
  genealogical and Confederate ancestral research.

- Talk to knowledgeable "old-timers" and local historians.

•Visit historic sites and Civil War battlefields.

•Read, read, read.

Conduct your research with an open mind, because people do make errors. From time to time, research materials will contain misspelled words, incorrect dates, and garbled facts. Original and copied documents, regardless of their age, will contain errors. For example, a 1905 copyist of Confederate records may have had difficulty in reading and transcribing original Civil War pay vouchers (as would we). Humans are subject to making errors, which can be counteracted by cross-referencing and documenting our research with valid sources. A cardinal rule: never assume that everything written, heard, or seen is the complete truth. It may only be a fragment or a clue in your research.

It is also important to maintain a positive mental attitude. During a particular research session at a state archives, I questioned an archivist about where specific information regarding an ancestor might be located. "You probably won't be able to find that," she responded. Yet the information I sought was on microfilm only a few feet from her desk. While most librarians and archivists are helpful, they cannot possibly be familiar with all sources, nor do they have the time to teach all patrons. It would have been unfortunate if I had accepted the answer and given up on my search. So, when a dead-end is encountered, do not allow negativism, frustration, or discouragement to set in; instead be positive, and rise to meet the challenge.

Develop a plan of action. For years, management professors have promoted the concept that results will increase with the establishment of defined goals and objectives. Good management techniques should also be applied to ancestral research. Begin your planning process by writing the questions (objectives) which you want answered. Are you interested in finding the names of great-great-grandparents and whether a family member served as a Confederate soldier? Would you like to identify his military unit and learn about the battles in which he fought? Are you interested in the valiant struggle of Confederate women, children, old people, and slaves on the homefront? Do you seek information about births, marriages, or places of burial? These are but a few questions open to a novice genealogist.

A variety of project assignments will produce interest and enthusiasm. Ancestral research should not be a dull job composed of mundane tasks, it should be an interesting, exhilarating experience! Interest will be sustained if a variety of activities are underway simultaneously.

Mrs. Sarah Mincey (second lady from the left on the back row), who lived to be 102 years old, often related to her family about the time when she nursed a wounded Confederate soldier who had straggled into her yard from the nearby battlefield at Chickamauga, Georgia. During the second day, she could hear from her country home the distant clash of armies, when suddenly a great roar rose above the din of battle. The wounded soldier began to scream the Rebel yell from his sick bed, and when the kind lady rushed to check on him, the soldier exclaimed "We've whipped 'em! We've whipped 'em!" What they had heard was Longstreet's breakthrough of the Federal lines, which ultimately led to the rout of Rosecrans' forces by the Army of Tennessee. *Photo Courtesy of the Author*

Patience will be rewarded. Enjoy yourself and work at your own steady pace. It is not necessary to work under self-imposed, strict guidelines. Maintain a relaxed, comfortable pace; and, above all, be patient with yourself and the projects on which you are working. Each book read, each challenge accepted, each project completed will bring you closer to discovering your Confederate ancestors.

The most difficult part in finding Confederate ancestors is getting started! It is easy to procrastinate, to fail to set aside time, and to waffle on the commitment; but if we only realize how easily accessible information is, we would start at once.

At this point, objectives and project ideas should be reduced to writing. The first objective should be to trace your family line to 1920 and to identify the location of family residences at that time. Information will be presented on the following pages on how to trace your family lineage to 1860. But the first step is locating your ancestors in 1920. Even if your Civil War forebears and their state and county of residence are already known, documentation and verification should still be done with source material.

Genealogists advise us to contact and interview older family members and longtime family friends. An interview should be simply a series of friendly questions designed to secure information in order to establish your family line. The gaps in family lines can be filled in later from other records. Information to be recorded from interviews should include:

- The names of forebears and their relatives

- Birth places, location of residences and burial sites

- Information about religious, military, and school
  affiliations

- Family "stories" from past generations and other
  information which will help you in identifying your
  ancestors

Oral history can provide a wealth of information, but it should be verified by other sources. If family members cannot be visited, try to telephone or write for information. Whenever you send query letters, include a self-addressed stamped envelope. If you are fortunate, you might discover that someone has already traced your family line.

Many Southern state libraries maintain collections of family histories.

IS ANCESTRAL RESEARCH EXPENSIVE?

No. A novice genealogist can use his or her home as a base of operations. The dining room table and kitchen phone are good starting points, but consideration should be given to the purchase of items which will aid in organization and collection of data. These items include:

- Three-ring binder notebooks, useful in the collection of genealogical data. Printed family charts to record family lineage are available from publishers, state archives, and genealogical societies.

- Cardboard boxes, useful for file storage. A quick retrieval of files is possible with an indexed filing system.

- Genealogical books may be borrowed from libraries. However, you will also want to build your own collection of books and manuals.

- A magnifying glass is a good investment to help read documents and view old photographs.

- Tape recorder and video and still cameras will add a greater dimension to your work.

A surprising amount of genealogical reference information is found in local libraries, and the local library and genealogical society of your ancestral county will yield a wealth of data. Items which are often available include published and unpublished family histories, society newsletters, maps and charts, newspapers, and a variety of valuable books. County histories are very important to research, and they may include hard-to-find Confederate company rolls of local volunteers. The interlibrary loan system provides access to out-of-print books and archival microfilm.

Family information is obtained by using official public documents, such as deeds, tax rolls, birth and death records, court records, marriage records, voting lists, wills, guardianship papers, orphans' records, professional fee books, divorce papers, estate documents, and asylum records. Public documents are usually found in county courthouses. The quantity and quality of these materials will vary greatly. The county court clerk's or the probate judge's office will offer assistance in reviewing these records. Local church materials, including membership rolls, baptismal records, and cemetery records are also very useful sources for genealogical information. Upon completion of your local research, you will be ready to begin work in a state archives to trace your family line back to 1860.

Federal census records will greatly assist you in establishing your Confederate "connection." This source is the single most valuable tool for the genealogist, and its usage should be mastered before proceeding with further research. If you wish to review your knowledge of the use of census records, information is given below.

THE FEDERAL POPULATION CENSUS RECORDS

The 1850 and 1860 census records are especially important, because they list the names, ages, sex, and birthplace for each person in the household. Prior to 1850, only the head of household was identified by name, while other family members appeared as numerical tallies under broad age and sex categories. Federal privacy laws restrict the public from viewing modern census records; that is, those recorded after 1920. So, the 1920 census is the most recent census available to the general public.

Some census records have been destroyed by war, fire, negligence, and acts of nature. The worst destruction occurred in 1921, when 99 percent of the 1890 census was lost to fire. For these "lost" census records in your state, other records may be substituted, such as tax rolls or state censuses.

HOW DO I FIND MY ANCESTOR IN THE 1920 CENSUS?

As previously explained, it is necessary to trace one's family to 1920 in order to make the connection with the federal census of that year. Thereafter, one can compare names and ages by moving back through earlier censuses to discover new heads of households (thus, new direct forebears). For example, your grandfather may have been two years old in the 1920 census, which shows the name of his father and mother and their ages. By consulting the 1910 census, you will not find your grandfather, but you should find his mother and father by name, only, roughly, ten years younger. Chart your family surnames, comparing names and ages with the 1900, 1880, 1870, 1860, and 1850 census records. The census for each decade will be arranged by state, county, and a subdivision component (township, militia district, or precinct). Private publishers print indexes for most state censuses. With this aid, you are able to go directly to the microfilm page where your family is enumerated. For later census records, a system called the Soundex Coding Guide has been developed to assist researchers, especially those unsure of where their ancestors lived from 1880 to 1920.

HOW WILL THIS INFORMATION HELP ME FIND MY CONFEDERATE ANCESTORS?

With the names and ages of those who lived during the 1860s, the researcher is able to research Confederate service records to learn if his ancestors served as soldiers, were exempted from duty, or performed other capacities. From the census records, calculate the ages of all males living between 1860 and 1865. If the ages fall between 15 and 50, a strong possibility exists that the male ancestor served in a Confederate military unit. While the majority of soldiers were volunteers, the Confederate government did enact draft laws. Men 18 to 35 years of age were conscripted as of September 27, 1862; and men 17 to 50 years old were drafted during February 1864. Non-conscripted older men and underage boys were used in state militia and/or home guard units, and as reserves for regular units. In the early years, draft exemptions did exist for overseers of twenty or more slaves and for ministers, teachers, pharmacists, and other skilled workers. Some men with physical disabilities were exempted, as well as the few who could furnish a substitute. Overall, an extremely high number of Southern males served in the military, and the odds are great that you will encounter an ancestor who served the Confederacy in some official capacity.

AVAILABLE CENSUS ON MICROFILM

    1790>First Census, 12 rolls
    1790>Printed, 3 rolls
    1800>Second Census, 52 rolls
    1810>Third Census, 71 rolls

1820>Fourth Census, 142 rolls

1830>Fifth Census, 201 rolls

1840>Sixth Census, 580 rolls

1850>Seventh Census, 1,009 rolls
(First census to name each individual within a household.)

1860>Eighth Census, 1,438 rolls

1870>Ninth Census, 1,748 rolls

1880>Tenth Census, 1,454 rolls
(Families with children ten years old or less are indexed on Soundex microfilm on a state-wide basis covering 47 states and territories.)

1890>Eleventh Census, 3 rolls
(Badly damaged by fire, these rolls are the only ones which are extant.)

1900>Twelfth Census, 1,784 rolls
(Soundex/Miracode microfilm has all families indexed for 21 states.)

WHAT INFORMATION IS FOUND IN FEDERAL POPULATION CENSUS RECORDS?

Since 1790, and for each decade thereafter, federal census records have proven to be a most valuable tool in tracking ancestry. Even with spelling mistakes and unrecorded gaps in data, these records provide an excellent basis for research, especially for those who have very little family information. With the name of an ancestor and the state of residence identified, one can begin to trace one's lineage.

The earliest census returns from 1790 to 1840 indicate the name of the family head. For other family members, however, there are no names recorded—only numerical tallies pinpointing age and sex categories. The 1850 census is a milestone, because it reveals the name and birthplace for *every* member in the household. This is a bonanza for ancestral researchers! In each of the succeeding decades, federal enumerators gathered more and more data. Listed below is a summary of information that can be drawn from the questions posed in each decennial census from 1790 to the 1920 census records:

> •1790>Name of head of household; numerical tallies show free white males, free white females, slaves, and other persons.

> •1800 and 1810>Name of head of household (if white, the age and sex are given); race; numerical tallies for slaves.

•1820>Name of head of household; age, sex, and race; numerical tallies for slaves, deaf and dumb, blind, and foreigners not naturalized.

•1830 and 1840>Name of head of household; age, sex, and race are given; numerical tallies identify number of deaf and dumb, blind, insane and idiotic (and whether in public or private charge), and slaves; number of persons employed in industry; and identifies literacy and pensioners for Revolutionary or other military service.

•1850>Names of each member counted in the family or as a part of the household; age, sex, and race; occupation; birthplace; additional information that could be checked if applicable–married within the year, attended school within the year, cannot read or write; identification if a pauper or convict and schedules for slaves and persons who died during the year.

•1860>Names of each member of household; age, sex, and race; occupation; birthplace; notation if parents were foreign-born; additional information that could be found if applicable–month of birth and month of marriage (if happened during the year); identification of deaf and dumb, blind, insane, idiotic, pauper, or convict; number of slave houses; supplemental schedules for slaves and persons who died during the year.

•1870>Names of each member of the household; age; race; occupation; value of real estate; value of personal estate; birthplaces; whether parents were foreign-born; month of birth if born within the year; month of marriage if married within the year; school attendance; literacy; whether deaf and dumb, blind, insane, or idiotic; male citizens 21 and over, and number of such persons denied the right to vote for reasons other than rebellion; supplemental schedules for persons who died during the year.

•1880>Names of each member of the household; address; relationship to family head; sex; race; age; marital status; month of birth if born within the census year; occupation; months unemployed during the year; sickness or temporary disability; whether blind, deaf and dumb, idiotic, insane, maimed, crippled, bedridden, or otherwise disabled; school attendance; literacy; birthplace of person and parents; supplemental schedules for persons who died during the year.

•1890>General schedules were destroyed by fire in Washington, D.C. Supplemental schedules for Union veterans and their widows have survived, however.

•1900>Names of each member of the household; address; relationship to family head; sex; race; age; marital status; number of children born and number now living; birthplace of person and parents; if foreign born, year of immigration and whether naturalized; occupation; months not employed; school attendance; literacy; ability to speak English; whether on a farm; home owned or rented and if owned, whether mortgaged.

•1910>Names of each member of the household; address; relationship to family head; sex; race; age; marital status; number of years of present marriage; for women, number of children born and number now living; birthplace and mother tongue of person and parents; if foreign born, year of immigration, whether naturalized, and whether able to speak English, or if not, language spoken; occupation, industry, and class of worker; if an employee, whether out of work during the year; literacy; school attendance; home owned or rented; if owned, whether mortgaged; whether farm or house; whether a survivor of Union or Confederate Army or Navy; whether blind, deaf and dumb.

•1920>Names of each member of the household; address; relationship to family head; sex; race; age; marital status; if foreign born, year of immigration to the U.S., whether naturalized, and year of naturalization; school attendance; literacy; birthplace of person and parents; mother tongue of foreign born; ability to speak English; occupation; industry, and class of worker; home owned or rented; if owned, whether free or mortgaged.

Printed census indexes list family names alphabetically. Identifying data such as the county of residence and household number allow the researcher to find easily the appropriate microfilm roll for viewing. The following index serves as an example:

INDEX TO 1860 FEDERAL CENSUS OF SOUTH CAROLINA

Code	No.	Name	Code	No.	Name	Code	No.
ORBG	343	Abney, Jerrot	EDFD	18	Adams, Ambrose	DLTN	475
ORBG	322	Abney, John K	EDFD	149	Adams, Anderson	RHLD	85
ORBG	340	Abney, John P	EDFD	156	Adams, Andrew	MRBO	195
ORBG	331	Abney, Joseph	EDFD	111	Adams, Ann	PKNS	68
ORBG	315	Abney, Martha	EDFD	159	Adams, Anney	RHLD	83
ORBG	340	Abney, Mrs. Dempsy	NWBY	250	Adams, Archy	LRNS	233
ORBG	335	Abney, Permelia*	EDFD	54	Adams, Benhn P	COTN	260
ORBG	313	Abney, Tabitha	EDFD	161	Adams, Benjamin	COTN	317
ORBG	336	Abney, William H*	EDFD	194	Adams, Benjamin W	COTN	301
ORBG	322	Abney, Wilson	EDFD	161	Adams, Benjeman	ABVL	103
CHFD	164	Abott, Isaac	FAFD	239	Adams, Bynahm	LCTR	204
ORBG	379	Abraham, S	CLDN	235	Adams, Catherine*	CHFD	118
ORBG	383	Abrahams, A H	CHTN	269	Adams, Charles C D	CHTN	434
PKNS	27	Abrahams, John	LRNS	320	Adams, Charlott	MARN	52
BNWL	478	Abrahams, Jos	LRNS	310	Adams, Cornelia**	PKNS	128
BNWL	478	Abrahams, Jos	LRNS	320	Adams, Cornelious*	CHTN	513
RHLD	88	Abrahams, Lewis	CLDN	200	Adams, Creero	EDFD	111
SPBG	341	Abrahams, Lydia	LRNS	321	Adams, D E	WMBG	315
PKNS	75	Abrahams, Thomas*	NWBY	242	Adams, D J*	EDFD	117
SPBG	309	Abrahams, Thos*	LRNS	320	Adams, D L	EDFD	84
RHLD	75	Abram, J*	DLTN	412	Adams, Daniel	NWBY	259
RHLD	67	Abrams, A F W**	CHTN	489	Adams, David A	YORK	421
RHLD	76	Abrams, A**	CHTN	314	Adams, Dr J F	EDFD	66
RHLD	82	Abrams, Benjn*	NWBY	285	Adams, Dr Wm	YORK	421
PKNS	30	Abrams, J M	COTN	333	Adams, E L	CHTN	363
CHTN	129	Abrams, J N*	NWBY	267	Adams, Elisabeth*	LCTR	200
DLTN	387	Abrams, John A	NWBY	287	Adams, Eliza	RHLD	85
SMTR	159	Abrams, Joseph**	NWBY	286	Adams, Eliza A*	ABVL	29
PKNS	54	Abrams, Joseph*	NWBY	286	Adams, Elizabeth	LCTR	159
PKNS	55	Abrams, Mary	NWBY	285	Adams, Elizabeth	UNON	223
PKNS	51	Abrams, R T B	WMBG	319	Adams, Elizabeth*	CHTN	435
SPBG	209	Abrams, Saml	NWBY	264	Adams, F*	CHFD	156
PKNS	72	Abrams, Thomas P	NWBY	275	Adams, F C Walker*	RHLD	28
PKNS	75	Abrams, William	FAFD	222	Adams, Frances	PKNS	68
DLTN	379	Abrams, Wilson*	NWBY	265	Adams, Frank	ABVL	42
PKNS	73	Abrams, Wm J	HORY	58	Adams, Franklin	ADSN	246
CHTN	303	Abrey, William*	GRVL	537	Adams, G P	CHTN	243
SPBG	308	Abshar, Joseph	YORK	589	Adams, Georgia*	ADSN	260
PKNS	73	Abstence, Hugh	BNWL	566	Adams, Grace**	CHTN	209
PKNS	73	Abstence, Susan	BNWL	583	Adams, Harmon	EDFD	137
PKNS	57	Abstence, William	BNWL	566	Adams, Henry	EDFD	149
CHTN	107	Accock, J M	UNON	275	Adams, Henry	NWBY	276
ABVL	36	Acher, Wm B*	ABVL	141	Adams, Hilmon	DLTN	379
CHTR	7	Acheson, Archbd*	CHTN	316	Adams, Hiram	EDFD	61
CHTR	71	Acker, Amos	ADSN	178	Adams, Hugh	CHTN	476
CHTN	385	Acker, C A	GRVL	428	Adams, Isaac	ADSN	216
LRNS	272	Acker, C P N	GRVL	423	Adams, J H	EDFD	144
LRNS	280	Acker, Holbert	ADSN	194	Adams, J H	YORK	367
LRNS	280	Acker, J J	ADSN	178	Adams, J H**	LCTR	159
LRNS	299	Acker, J S	ADSN	188	Adams, J Leander	YORK	422
LRNS	278	Acker, Mariah	ADSN	210	Adams, J M	PKNS	78
LRNS	271	Acker, Peter G	ADSN	165	Adams, J M	ADSN	249
LRNS	335	Acker, Rebecca	ADSN	308	Adams, J P	LRNS	264
LRNS	271	Acker, Robt	ADSN	178	Adams, J Q	EDFD	86
LRNS	278	Acker, Wm H	ADSN	194	Adams, J R	ADSN	178
LRNS	279	Ackerman, Augt*	CHTN	202	Adams, J S	LCTR	158
LRNS	266	Ackerman, David	COTN	317	Adams, J T	EDFD	86
LRNS	280	Ackerman, Ed M	COTN	314	Adams, J W	UNON	227
LRNS	264	Ackerman, Eliza	COTN	315	Adams, J W	EDFD	144
LRNS	266	Ackerman, Frank*	CHTN	202	Adams, J W T	LCTR	158
LRNS	266	Ackerman, Hy W	COTN	313	Adams, Jackson	MRBO	198
ADSN	263	Ackerman, James S*	COTN	295	Adams, James	ABVL	145
ADSN	178	Ackerman, John G	COTN	315	Adams, James	CHTR	3
SPBG	223	Ackerman, Lorenzo	COTN	317	Adams, James	ADSN	205
SPBG	349	Ackerman, Mary	COTN	315	Adams, James	COTN	268
SPBG	349	Ackerman, R W	COTN	350	Adams, James	MRBO	185
YORK	450	Ackerman, S O	COTN	315	Adams, James	NWBY	278
SPBG	350	Ackerman, Sylvester	COTN	313	Adams, James	FAFD	245
SPBG	227	Ackers, Louisa*	CHTN	242	Adams, James H	RHLD	84
YORK	391	Acock, James	CHTN	141	Adams, James L	EDFD	129
YORK	391	Acock, Jane	YORK	402	Adams, James M	LCTR	196
SPBG	223	Acock, John C	YORK	386	Adams, James P	RHLD	23
CHTR	67	Acock, Joseph	UNON	232	Adams, James U	RHLD	92
MARN	101	Acock, Mary*	BUFT	59	Adams, Jane	CHFD	131
MARN	102	Actepie, C B*	CHTN	491	Adams, Jas	LRNS	275

PRINTED CENSUS INDEX
Courtesy Georgia Department of Archives and History

1	2	3	4	5	6	7	8	9	10	11	12	13	14	15	16	17
1			Sarah	21	F	W	K.H.			Ala						
2			Mary	4	F	W				Ala						
3			Amitta	1	F	W				"						
4			J.W. Romans	9	M	W	At Home			"						
5			Richmond	8	M	W	"			"						
6	284	285	Daly John	37	M	W	Farmer		125	Ala						
7			Mary A	36	F	W	K.H.			Ga						
8			Charlotte	14	F	W	At School			"						
9			Peter P	12	M	W	"			"						
10			William	8	M	W	"			"						
11			Solomon	3	M	W				"						
12			Sarah	11/12	F	W				Ala			Ala				
13	285	286	Beaty J.X.	49	M	W	Farmer	300	250	S.C.						
14			Mary	46	F	W	K.H.			Ga						
15			Martha	20	F	W	At School			Ala						
16			Mary	11	F	W	"			"						
17			Nichols John	16	M	W	Farm L.			"						
18	286	287	Smith S.S.	26	M	W	Farmer		100	Ga						
19			Frances	24	F	W	K.H.			Ala						
20			Frances	2	F	W				"						
21			Charles	1	M	W				"						
22	287	288	Hunt Gilbert	24	M	W	Farmer	250	250	"						
23			Amina	22	F	W	K.H.			Ga						
24			William	2	M	W				Ala						
25	288	289	Freeman Eli	70	M	W	Miller	100	100	S.C.						
26			Mary	50	F	W	K.H.			"						
27			Texas	18	F	W	At Home			Ala						
28			Janie	15	M	W				Ala						

RANDOLPH COUNTY, ALABAMA, CENSUS ROLL, 1870

These rolls are not always easy to read. Use a magnifying glass and hand copy information for later use. *Courtesy Alabama Department of Archives and History*

THE REGIONAL SYSTEM OF THE NATIONAL ARCHIVES

In 1969, the regional archives system was established in order to make historically valuable federal records accessible to the general public in their own geographic areas. Aside from a multitude of preserved records, some 50,000 rolls of are available at each microfilm research facility across the county. Among the topics of special interest to Confederate genealogists are war and military records, federal population censuses, and land records. Special programs offered to the public include workshops, exhibits, educational films, guidance on archival procedures, speakers, and tours.

LOCATIONS

•**National Archives-New England Region**
380 Trapelo Road Waltham, MA 02154
617-647-8100
[Connecticut, Maine, Massachusetts, New Hampshire, Rhode Island, Vermont]

•**National Archives-Northeast Region**
Building 22 - Military Ocean Terminal
Bayonne, NJ 07002-5388
201-823-7252
[New Jersey, New York, Puerto Rico, the Virgin Islands]

•**National Archives-Mid Atlantic Region**
9th and Market Streets, Room 1350
Philadelphia, PA 19107
215-597-3000
[Delaware, Pennsylvania, Maryland, Virginia, West Virginia]

•**National Archives-Southeast Region**
1557 St. Joseph Avenue
East Point, GA 30344
404-763-7477
[Alabama, Georgia, Florida, Kentucky, Mississippi, North Carolina, South Carolina, Tennessee]

•**National Archives-Great Lakes Region**
7358 South Pulaski Road
Chicago, IL 60629
312-581-7816
[Illinois, Indiana, Michigan, Minnesota, Ohio, Wisconsin]

•**National Archives-Central Plains Region**
2312 East Bannister Road
Kansas City, MO 64131
816-926-6272
[Iowa, Kansas, Missouri, Nebraska]

•**National Archives-Southwest Region**
501 West Felix Street, P.O. Box 6216
Ft. Worth, TX 76115
817-334-5525
[Arkansas, Louisiana, New Mexico, Oklahoma, Texas]

•**National Archives-Rocky Mountain Region**
Building 48-Denver Federal Center
Denver, CO 80225-0307
303-236-0817
[Colorado, Montana, North Dakota, South Dakota, Utah, Wyoming]

•**National Archives-Pacific Sierra Region**
1000 Commodore Drive
San Bruno, CA 94066
415-876-9009
[Northern California, Hawaii, Nevada (except Clark County), American Samoa, the Trust Territory of the Pacific Islands]

•**National Archives-Pacific Southwest Region**
24000 Avila Road, P.O. Box 6719
Laguna Niguel, CA 92607-6719
714-643-4241
[Southern California, Arizona, and Clark County, Nevada]

•**National Archives-Pacific Northwest Region**
6125 Sand Point Way NE
Seattle, WA 98115
206-526-6507
[Idaho, Oregon, Washington]

•**National Archives-Alaska Region**
654 West Third Avenue
Anchorage, AK 99501
907-271 -244 1
[Alaska]

GENEALOGICAL FORMS

Before proceeding with your Confederate research, you should obtain certain genealogical forms and charts which will assist you in recording and organizing family information. These forms are available for purchase through genealogical societies and private companies, and they are found in genealogy workbooks sold in major bookstores. Printed forms and charts may vary slightly in format, but all serve equally well.

Example 1

The FAMILY GROUP SHEET is a basic form used to record information about one single family. Each member of the household will have their full name, dates of birth and death, marriage data, and locations of residences.

Example 2

The ANCESTRAL CHART shows direct lineage in a line format. Only the direct lineage line (parents, grandparents, great-grandparents, etc.) is entered. Each name listed could also have a family group sheet which provides information on all other family members not appearing in the direct lineage line.

Example 3

The FAMILY RELATIONSHIP CHART enables the researcher to determine the relationship to another person when both share a common ancestor.

Example 4

A completed FAMILY GROUP SHEET and all other forms are illustrated on the following pages.

FAMILY GROUP CHART

HUSBAND
Born _____ Place _____
Chr. _____ Place _____
Marr. _____ Place _____
Died _____ Place _____
Bur. _____ Place _____
Husband's Father _____
Husband's Mother _____

WIFE
Born _____ Place _____
Chr. _____ Place _____
Died _____ Place _____
Bur. _____ Place _____
Wife's Father _____
Wife's Mother _____

Husband _____
Wife _____
SOURCES OF INFORMATION:
NAME AND ADDRESS OF COMPILER:

SEX M-F	CHILDREN List in order of birth	WHEN BORN			WHERE BORN			TO WHOM MARRIED	WHEN MARR.			WHEN DIED			WHERE BURIED		
		Day	Month	Year	Town	County	State		Day	Month	Year	Day	Month	Year	Town	County	State
1																	
2																	
3																	
4																	
5																	
6																	
7																	
8																	
9																	
10																	
11																	
12																	

EXAMPLE 1: THE FAMILY GROUP SHEET
Courtesy Georgia Department of Archives and History

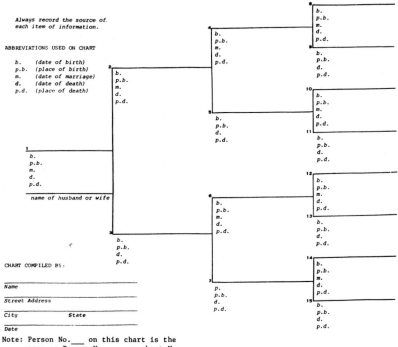

Always record the source of each item of information.

ABBREVIATIONS USED ON CHART

b.   (date of birth)
p.b. (place of birth)
m.   (date of marriage)
d.   (date of death)
p.d. (place of death)

CHART COMPILED BY :

Name

Street Address

City   State

Date

Note: Person No.___ on this chart is the
      same as Person No. ___ on chart No.___

EXAMPLE 2: THE ANCESTRAL CHART
Courtesy Georgia Department of Archives and History

Your lineage ⟶

Relative's lineage

COMMON ANCESTOR	CHILD	GRAND CHILD	GREAT GRAND CHILD	2ND GREAT GRAND CHILD	3RD GREAT GRAND CHILD
CHILD	BROTHER/SISTER	AUNT/UNCLE OR NEPHEW/NIECE	GREAT AUNT/UNCLE OR NEPHEW/NIECE	2ND GREAT AUNT/UNCLE OR NEPHEW/NIECE	3RD GREAT AUNT/UNCLE OR NEPHEW/NIECE
GRAND CHILD	AUNT/UNCLE OR NEPHEW/NIECE	FIRST COUSIN	FIRST COUSIN, ONCE REMOVED	FIRST COUSIN, TWICE REMOVED	FIRST COUSIN, 3 TIMES REMOVED
GREAT GRAND CHILD	GREAT AUNT/UNCLE OR NEPHEW/NIECE	FIRST COUSIN ONCE REMOVED	SECOND COUSIN	SECOND COUSIN, ONCE REMOVED	SECOND COUSIN, TWICE REMOVED
2ND GREAT GRAND CHILD	2ND GREAT AUNT/UNCLE OR NEPHEW/NIECE	FIRST COUSIN, TWICE REMOVED	SECOND COUSIN, ONCE REMOVED	THIRD COUSIN	THIRD COUSIN, ONCE REMOVED
3RD GREAT GRAND CHILD	3RD GREAT AUNT/UNCLE OR NEPHEW/NIECE	FIRST COUSIN, 3 TIMES REMOVED	SECOND COUSIN, TWICE REMOVED	THIRD COUSIN, ONCE REMOVED	FOURTH COUSIN

EXAMPLE 3: FAMILY RELATIONSHIP CHART

In order to determine your relationship to a relative, enter the name of the common ancestor in the top left block. Next, enter names of your lineage from the common ancestor horizontally. Then, enter the names of your relative's lineage from the common ancestor. Your relationship will be shown in the block that intersects both your name and that of the relative. *Courtesy Georgia Genealogical Society*

HUSBAND Joseph Crandal Bailey
Born 30 Nov. 1832   **Place** Marietta, Cobb County, Georgia
Chr.   **Place**
Marr. 1850   **Place** 1850 Randolph County Alabama Census says married during year.
Died 28 Sept. 1897   **Place** Randolph County Alabama
Bur. Sept. 1897   **Place** Union Hill Baptist Church + Cemetery; Roanoke, Randolph Co., Ala.
HUSBAND'S FATHER Patrick B. Bailey   **HUSBAND'S MOTHER**
HUSBAND'S OTHER WIVES Mary Emma Stewart m. 5 July 1896 Randolph Co., Ala.

WIFE Mary Ann "Polly Ann" Kilgore
Born 3 June 1834   **Place** Georgia
Chr.   **Place**
Died 5 Jan. 1895   **Place** Randolph County, Alabama
Bur. Jan. 1895   **Place** Union Hill Baptist Church + Cemetery; Roanoke, Randolph Co., Ala.
WIFE'S FATHER Peter Kilgore Jr. b. 10 Sept. 1798 North Car.   **WIFE'S MOTHER** Charlotte "Lottie" Segars
WIFE'S OTHER HUSBANDS

SEX M/F	CHILDREN — List each child (whether living or dead) in order of birth — Given Names / Surname	WHEN BORN — DAY / MONTH / YEAR	WHERE BORN — TOWN	COUNTY	STATE OR COUNTRY	DATE OF FIRST MARRIAGE — TO WHOM	WHEN DIED — DAY / MONTH / YEAR
1 F	Charlotte France Bailey	20 May 1856		Randolph	Ala.	"Sis Edwards" Samuel J. Edwards	4 Sept. 1939
2 m	Peter Patrick Bailey	5 May 1859		"	"	Martha Arene "Aunt Rene" Vinson	29 Oct. 1934
3 m	William Thomas Bailey	29 May 1862		"	"	Josephine Richardson	24 Apr. 1892 13 Mar. 1946
4 m	Soloman Henry Jeremiah Bailey	28 May 1867		"	"	Martha Odulia Henry	1946
5 F	Sarah Amanda "Mandy" Bailey	9 Dec. 1869		"	"	John Wesley White	1953
6 m	John B. Bailey	1871		"	"	Sarah Bulah White	
7							
8							
9							
10							
11							

SOURCES OF INFORMATION
Family Bible page owned by Jerry + Carolyn Evans, Fairburn, Ga.
1850, 1860, 1870, 1880 Randolph Co., Ala. Census
Pension Records of Joseph Bailey 9th Ga. Regt. Ballation.
Death Records of Randolph Co., Ala.
Family Church + Cemetery; (Union Hill) Roanoke, Randolph Co., Ala.
  John Wesley + Sarah Bulah White are brother + sister.
All but first 2 children are buried at Union Hill.

OTHER MARRIAGES
Joseph married 2nd to Mary Emma Stewart
          5 July 1896
  Information from pension records of Joseph.
Pension records are at the Ala. archives.

EXAMPLE 4: A COMPLETED FAMILY GROUP SHEET
Courtesy of Linda Adams

GENEALOGICAL RESEARCH AT A GLANCE:

FAMILY HISTORY

NATIONAL ARCHIVES: Census,
military, & federal records

STATE ARCHIVES: State & County
records, genealogical collections

COUNTY COURTHOUSES: Public records–birth,
marriage, death, tax, & estate

COMMUNITY SOURCES: Public Libraries, Historical
& Genealogical Societies–special collections,
family histories, & county histories

RELATIVES AS SOURCES: Interview older relatives &
family friends, seek genealogical charts, & listen
for family "stories"

HOME SOURCES: Family bibles, official papers, photos,
scrapbooks, marriage licenses, school records, letters

START WITH YOURSELF: Jot down names, dates, places, & kinship

---

J. H. Segars Model ©1996

The process of conducting genealogical research does not have to be complicated or difficult. The secret of tracing one's lineage and recording family histories is quite simple: review as many good sources as possible. The end result is a documented, compiled genealogy.

★ DISCOVERING CONFEDERATE RECORDS ★

The Civil War is for the American imagination, the greatest single event of our history. Without too much wrenching, it may, in fact, be said to be American history.
—Robert Penn Warren

Now that you have identified a Confederate ancestor, you are ready to explore the fascinating historical records which might reveal his regiment, battle service, wounds, imprisonment, and perhaps his physical characteristics. Surprisingly, a vast amount of material survived the war, and thousands of volumes are available for studying the conflict. As you explore Confederate records, you will be constantly directed to additional sources. The subject is captivating and your research will be a legacy for your descendants. All history begins with the individual. As you gather information about a specific ancestor and his family, you will begin to understand what was happening in their town, county, or state, and how those events fit into the larger drama we call American history. This learning process will undoubtedly reveal to you the heroism, suffering, and fortitude of those whom we are proud to call our Confederate ancestors.

CONFEDERATE ARCHIVES

An abundance of materials from the Confederate States archives has been preserved, stored, and eventually microfilmed by the U.S. government. Although much of the material deals with the various governmental departments, we can find, in muster rolls and other documents, information about our military and civilian ancestors. *The Guide to the Archives of the Confederate States of America* by Henry Pitney Beers, a National Archives publication, provides a detailed study of these records. Beers describes the collection and compilation of these sources as follows:

> Before the Confederate Government evacuated Richmond some of its archives were moved southward. . . . During 1864 some Government bureaus moved to more southern cities and in March 1865 the Government agencies in Richmond shipped records from the Capital over the Richmond and Danville Railroad.

On April 2, 1865, the Union Army penetrated the defenses of Petersburg, forcing a Confederate retreat from the southern approach to Richmond. On that day President Davis directed all department heads to complete arrangements for leaving the Capital. Some records were then boxed for rail transportation; clerks piled up other records in the streets and set them afire and other records were simply abandoned in the Government offices. Some records were saved by Union Army officers who entered the city and some were carried off by soldiers and individuals. Government offices were set aflame and most of the buildings that had been occupied by Confederate Government departments and agencies were destroyed along with quantities of records.

On occupying Richmond and other points in the South, the U.S. Army seized considerable quantities of Confederate records and sent them to the War Department at Washington.

In later years the Office of the Secretary of War and the Adjutant General's Office had custody of the Confederate Archives. In 1881 the Archive Office was merged into the Record Division of the Office of the Secretary of War.

The offices having custody of the Confederate archives undertook to make them more usable for searches regarding claimants and pension applicants and to facilitate the publishing work of the War Records Office. The Archives Division classified the bound volumes roughly according to provenance into groups designated "chapters," the volumes numbered serially in each chapter. The volumes are still arranged on the shelves in the National Archives according to this classification and the chapters are as follows:

> I. Adjutant and Inspector General's Department
> II. Military Commands
> III. Engineer Department
> IV. Ordnance Department
> V. Quartermaster General's Department
> VI. Medical Department
> VII. Legislative Records
> VIII. Miscellaneous Reeords
> IX. Office of the Secretary of War
> X. Treasury Department
> XI. Post Office Department
> XII. Judiciary

A subject index to the collection is available and later it became desirable to acquire additional reeords, particularly the records of Confederate Army commands.

NOTE: The detailed and voluminous material of the Confederate archives is primarily used by scholars and experienced researchers. The following Compiled Military Service records, based on original records, will be the easiest and best source to consult for information on individuals.

COMPILED MILITARY SERVICE RECORDS

In the years following the war, personnel at the U.S. War Department were frequently called upon to furnish transcripts of Confederate military records. These requests came from individuals, state officials, claims commissions, historical societies, patriotic groups, and veterans' organizations. There was a growing need to preserve the original reeords and yet make them available to researchers for ready reference.

In 1903, Congress passed an act authorizing the War Department to compile a complete roster of the officers and enlisted men of the Union and Confederate Armies from official records held by the government. The governors of several Confederate states were also persuaded to provide existing state Confederate personnel records to be copied for the project. In some cases, like Tennessee, the original records were never returned. Clerks were hired to copy data by hand from the original files to printed index cards. While little genealogical data is recorded on these cards, a wealth of valuable military information–including capsule unit histories, enlistments, absences, discharges, hospitalizations, deaths, captivity, rank, and identification of the military organization–is found. Following the index cards are copies of original one-name documents drawn from the files of the Confederate War Department. Enlisted men may or may not have original papers, while officers' records could have many documents attached. The actual carding and compilation was not completed until the late 1920s, with over nine million cards filed. Thus, the "compiled" military service records were devised to replace the aged and dilapidated originals; and now, through microfilm, are available to the public for researching Confederate ancestors.

The Compiled Service Records for the Confederate Army, Navy, and Marine personnel (and some civilians) can be found at the National Archives. Some of the microfilm series are available at National Archives branches, state archives, and research libraries. The microfilm series includes:

- •Indexes and the compiled service records of Confederate volunteers from each of the southern states.

- •Indexes and the compiled service records of Confederates who served in organizations raised directly by the Confederate government.

- Compiled records showing service records of military units in Confederate service.

- Copies of records of Confederate General Staff officers and nonregimental enlisted men.

- Subject file of the Confederate States Navy, 1861-1865.
  [Note: The series, *Muster Rolls and Payrolls of Ships and Shore Establishment of the Confederate Navy*, arranged by ship and establishment, is not on microfilm.]

- Index to letters received from Confederate civilians to the Confederate Seretary of War, Adjutant, Inspector General, and Quartermaster (and the letters).

- Confederate papers relating to citizens or business firms.

- Amnesty oaths relating to individuals, 1863-66.
  [Note: The U.S. government offered pardon or amnesty to southerners who took an oath of allegiance.]

- Case files of applications from former Confederates for Presidential pardons, 1865-67.

- U.S. Southern Claims Commission Reports.
  [Note: During 1871-80, this commission examined claims for property and services rendered to the U.S. Army by southern citizens who remained loyal to the Union; some claims to loyalty could be questionable and many were denied. These claims have been indexed and printed in two volumes: G. B. Mills, *Civil War Claims in the South* (Laguna Hills, CA, 1980).]

HOW WILL I LOCATE INFORMATION ABOUT MY ANCESTOR IN THE COMPILED MILITARY SERVICE RECORDS ON MICROFILM?

The general index to the records lists soldiers by state and surname in alphabetical order. The general index card for the individual soldier identifies the military unit. The microfilm roll for the military unit holds the record cards for the soldier, also found in alphabetical order by surname.

HOW MAY I OBTAIN COPIES OF MY ANCESTOR'S COMPILED SERVICE RECORDS?

They may be obtained by visiting a state archives, a National Archives Branch, or any other repository that holds the microfilm records. Duplication is possible on site through the use of special microfilm reader/printers. The charge per copy is nominal. If you wish to have the searching and photocopying done for you by staff members, the name of your ancestor's military unit must be provided. The National Archives will perform this service upon receipt of NATF (National Archives Trust Board) Form 80. You may obtain the necessary form by writing the Military Service Branch, National Archives and Records Administration, 7th and Pennsylvania Avenue, N.W., Washington, D.C. 20408. Your request for records will be verified by the Archives before you are asked to forward payment.

WHAT SHOULD I DO IF MY ANCESTOR DOES NOT APPEAR IN THE COMPILED SERVICE RECORDS?

Do not be discouraged. Remember that every soldier who served the Confederacy may not have a Compiled Service Record. Most state militia and home guard units were never entered on regular troop muster rolls. Moreover, many of the rosters of state organizations were lost or destroyed during the war or shortly thereafter; some were destroyed even because of the fear of retaliation by Federal troops during Reconstruction days.

If you are unable to find your ancestor listed on the index cards of the Compiled Service Records, do not give up your search! Check sources which list names of men who served in state and local units, as well as county records, which can be found at the state archives and/or county courthouses.

Do not give up if you are unable to locate the military service record of an ancestor. For example, the editor of this volume spent years as a novice family historian, trying to identify the military service of an ancestor, who was identified as Col. Henry L. Claiborne, but whose military record could not be verified in the *Official Records*. Through local histories of Nashville, newspapers, and militia records, he finally was able to confirm that Claiborne was indeed a colonel commanding the 88th Tennessee Infantry, a state unit; that he was a banker, who helped evacuate the Bank of Tennessee and the State Archives during the fall of Confederate

Nashville; and that his services had been commended by no other then Gen. Nathan Bedford Forrest!

EXAMPLES OF GENERAL INDEX CARDS
Courtesy Georgia Department of Archives and History

COMPILED SERVICE RECORD
Data found on Individual Card

(Confederate.)

| Cobb's Legion. | **Ga.** |

W. R. Segars

Pvt. { Co. ___ (Cavalry Battalion),
Cobb's Legion, Georgia Volunteers.

Appears on

Company Muster Roll

of the organization named above,

for _____ *Jan. + Feb.* _____, 1864.

Enlisted :
When _____ *Mch. 2*, 1863.
Where _____ *Decatur*
By whom _____ *Maj. Hardee*
Period _____

Last paid :
By whom _____ *Capt. Williams*
To what time _____ *Jan. 1*, 1864.

Amount of pay for horse, $ _____ *24* 100

Present or absent _____ *Present*

Remarks _____ *Detailed as shoe ma-*
ker Oct. 16, 1863

Cobb's Legion, Georgia Volunteers, was organized in August, 1861, as the Georgia Legion, and consisted of an infantry battalion of seven companies and a cavalry battalion of four companies. By S. O. No. 87, A. & I. G. O., dated April 10, 1863, it was directed that the infantry battalion and the cavalry battalion be separated into distinct organizations and each raised to a regiment, which order does not appear to have been carried out, except that the number of cavalry companies was increased. By S. O. No. 161, A. & I. G. O., dated July 11, 1864, the cavalry companies were directed to be designated the 9th Regiment Georgia Cavalry, but these companies appear to have continued to serve as a part of Cobb's Legion without change of designation.

Book mark : _____

(642) _____ *E. E. Rambler*
Copyist.

Card Identification:
Beginning letter of soldier's last name/ regiment/state

Soldier's name, rank, company, name of regiment

Inclusive dates of report or dates soldier is listed oncompany muster rolls

Date and location of enlistment; name of enrolling officer

Date of payment & disbursement officer

Amount of pay, presence or absence for duty noted, & remarks; in this case special duty & dates are recorded

Brief summary of the historyof the unit

Signature of the Federal copyist/clerk

Courtesy Georgia Department of Archives and History

A traveling photographer captured this 1898 image of one of Wade Hampton's horsemen–William R. Segars, Jr. Although this aged gentleman survived the war, his sixteen-year-old son and seventeen- year-old nephew did not. Also, his son-in-law, Isaac Burson, was killed near Resaca, leaving eight children fatherless. *Photo Courtesy of the Author*

Since copy clerks sometimes had difficulty reading names from the original muster rolls., the names of some soldiers are misspelled or entered under duplicate sets of records with different spellings. The "remarks" data provide information that might not be found elsewhere. It is always a good idea to verify data with other sources. The cards provide the unit identification that is necessary for research. If the soldier has a common name, and multiple records appear, extended genealogical research in pension files or other records will be warranted. Some researchers mistakenly assume that these copied index cards are original records, rather than containing information that has been copied from original Confederate documents, such as muster rolls, hospital lists, etc.

Courtesy Alabama Department of Archives and History

A Compiled Service Record will yield information on a soldier's capture and imprisonment, and may indicate whether he appeared on hospital muster rolls. In the above example, Pvt. Thomas G. Adams, of the 44th Georgia Infantry, was captured at Spotsylvania on May 10, 1864, received at Fort Delaware on May 20, 1864, exchanged with other prisoners on March 7, 1865, and transferred to the Jackson Confederate Hospital, Richmond,Virginia, on March 16, 1865.

Courtesy Georgia Department of Archives and History

Official Confederate documents, such as pay vouchers, will follow the index card abstracts for some soldiers. Officers might have several documents in their records, while privates often have none. The prize from these documents is the ancestor's signature. In this example, a cavalry private drew $24 for his services during March-April 1864. *Courtesy Georgia Department of Archives and History*

This original Confederate document appears in the Compiled Service Records of Pvt. Wiley T. Henry, who was discharged for disability on November 8, 1863, by order of Gen. Braxton Bragg, Army of Tennessee. The document indicates Private Henry's birthplace, describes his disability, and provides information that was otherwise unknown: that he was 5'8" tall, fair-complexioned, had light hair, blue eyes, and that he worked as a farmer before he enlisted. *Courtesy Georgia Department of Archives and History*

Martha H. Bailey (front row, seated), daughter of Pvt. Wiley T. Henry, who served with Co. A, 2nd Btn., Alabama Volunteer Infantry, is shown in this family photograph taken in Wedowee, Alabama, ca. 1919. Mrs. Bailey told the family that her father survived the War for Southern Independence after being disabled with deafness. On February 25, 1890, Henry was in the process of hitching a mule to a wagon for the trip to town, when the mule kicked him in the head, killing him instantly. Private Henry's Compiled Service Record is shown on the preceding page. *Photo Courtesy of Linda Adams*

CONFEDERATE PENSION RECORDS

Pension records located in state archives are a major source of information on individual soldiers, though many veterans were not eligible and/or did not apply for a pension. The U.S. government understandably refused to pay benefits to anyone except Union veterans, while the southern states accepted applications from resident Confederate veterans without regard to their original state of service. The earliest payments were for artificial limbs. (For example, the lion's share of the state budget for Mississippi in 1866 was expended on prostheses for needy Confederate veterans.) Later payments provided meagre relief to those most in need: the disabled, infirm, or indigent veteran or his widow.

Pension applications provide information about a soldier's military unit, hospitalization, imprisonment, military service, and even prewar occupation. Sometimes they include affidavits and marriage certificates from county officials, physicians, friends, Confederate veterans, and family members. The narratives might also reveal details about how the soldier came to be wounded, captured, and/or disabled.

CEMETERY, HOSPITAL, AND PRISONER OF WAR DATA

Countless Confederate ancestors who have been "forgotten" or "lost" to their descendants could be found by checking extant cemetery, hospital, and prisoner of war records. Soldiers often were buried where they died–near battlefields, old hospital sites, and prisoner of war camps. Many men have headstones which cannot be read or are missing; however, their names may still appear on cemetery lists. *The Register of Soldiers and Sailors Who Died in Federal Prisons and Military Hospitals in the North*, compiled in 1912 by the U S. War Department, is a valuable published source. Confederate prisoners of war died in staggering numbers in Northern camps. In his *Handbook of the Civil War*, William H. Price lists the figure as 26,000, compared to 30,200 Union deaths in Confederate prisoner of war camps. Other authors calculate southern deaths as higher than northern soldiers. As a percentage of prisoners held by each side or as a proportion of the armies involved, southern fatalities far exceeded their northern counterparts. Much has been written about Andersonville, but little is published about the unspeakable conditions at federally-operated Point Lookout, Camp Douglas, Fort Delaware, or Elmira. A study of the U.S. government's treatment of southern prisoners of war, its refusal to accept sick Federal inmates from Confederate prison camps, and its reluctance to exchange prisoners, is quite shocking.

A 1902 photograph of Capt. R. C. Hardison and his wife, Nannie, whom the residents of the Tennessee Confederate Soldiers' Home described as their "guardian angel . . . , her patient and long suffering was that of a Christian martyr." *From Confederate Veteran Magazine*

Questions for Witnesses as to Service of Husband and Marriage

STATE OF GEORGIA,

......Gwinnett.................... COUNTY

Personally before me comes ....J. I. Green................who, after being duly sworn, true answers to make to the following questions, answers as follows:

1. What is your name and where do you reside? Lawrenceville, Ga. Rt. 1 Gwinnett Co.

2. How long and since when have you known ...Mrs. Lucinda E. Jordon...... applicant?
Practically all her life.

3. How long and since when has she continuously resided in this State? (Give date.)
Ever since known her about all her life.

4. When and to whom was she married?...................How do you know?.........

5. How long and since when did you know ...James T. Jordon.............. her husband? Since 1862.

6. When and where did ......James T. Jordon......... the husband of applicant, die? May 27th, 1915. Gwinnett County, Georgia.

7. Were the applicant and her husband living together as husband and wife at the date of his death?
Yes.

8. If not, how long did they live apart before his death? ----------
Were they divorced? ----------

9. When, where and in what Company and Regiment did .....James T. Jordon...... enlist?
April 1862. Stone Mountain, Ga. Company "C" 12th Ga. Batt. Artillery.

10. Were you a member of the same Company? Yes.

11. How long within your personal knowledge did he perform actual military service with his Company and Regiment? April 1862, until 19th day of October 1864.

12. When and where did his Command surrender, and was discharged?
Near Petersburg, Va.

13. Were you personally present when it was surrendered? No.......If not, where were you Home, Lawrenceville, Ga, and how came you there? Wounded, being shot thru left thigh in battle Cedar Creek, Oct 19th, 1864. was given furlough home from Hospital on account of wounds for thirty days, not able to further serv

14. Was the husband of applicant personally present at surrender? No.......If not where was he? Home, Lawrenceville, Ga.........When, where and for what cause did he leave Command? (Give date) October 19th, 1864.........By whose authority did he leave his Command? Wounded Oct 19, 1864, being shot, And how long was he granted leave? thru neck, thirty days furlough thirty days......How do you know all this? Both wounded same day and received furlough for 30 days same time.

15. For what cause, if you know of your own knowledge, was he prevented from returning to his Command? Account of wound thru neck, never able to do further service.

16. What effort did he make to return to his Command and how do you know this? Of your own knowledge or how? Not able for further service after wounded.

Sworn to and subscribed before me this the
....27th..day of ..October............19 19} J. I. Green
......W. G. Robinson Ordinary }
of ......Gwinnett............. County }

(SEAL)

The foregoing example of a Confederate veteran's pension application, filed in the state of Georgia in 1919 by the veteran's widow, gives information concerning the wounds received by the soldier at the battle of Cedar Creek. The widow was granted the pension, based on documentation proving that the soldier was indeed in Confederate service and wounded. A copy of the couple's marriage certificate is also now on microfilm. *Courtesy Georgia Department of Archives and History*

Some headstones display Confederate service identification or a marker showing the United Daughters of the Confederacy's Cross of Honor. If Confederate military service is not shown, there are other clues to be found in inscribed verse, poetry, or death dates. For example, chiseled into a Barrow County, Georgia, headstone is the inscription "A brave spirit is buried here, who died a glorious death in his countrys cause." The birth and death dates (August 21, 1848, and September 27, 1865) reveal that the person was young, but how could it be determined that he was a soldier? Many sources, including the Compiled Service Records, were checked and yielded nothing about him. But an out-of-print county history book listed men who had served in a state militia unit from the area, and the name of the brave lad appeared on that list! Although little documentation exists for this individual's military service, a Confederate soldier is undoubtedly buried under a headstone erected by his loving family. What documentation could be better?

Anyone who locates a poorly-marked or unmarked grave of a Confederate soldier (or any American veteran) can order a quality marker free of charge from the U.S. government. For information, contact the Veterans Administration, Monument Service, 810 Vermont Avenue, Washington, D.C. 20420.

Locating and observing the grave of a Confederate ancestor is an educational and spiritual experience. If an ancestor is known to have served during the 1860s, and the grave is not located, then there could be a good reason, as exemplified in the following personal experience.

> While reading a local history book about an ancestral county, I noticed the name of a forebear listed as a member of a Confederate company from the area. Curiously, I had been searching for his grave with no success and was baffled that he was not buried with other family members in the family cemetery. I then began to search the Compiled Service Records microfilm; and, to my astonishment, the ancestor was shown to be in Vaughn's Brigade of the Department of Western Virginia and East Tennessee. He had been captured on October 28, 1864, in Jefferson County, Tennessee; transported to Louisville, Kentucky; and on November 26, arrived at Camp Douglas, Illinois. Slowly, I cranked the microfilm viewer, afraid to read the next frame because I knew the probable . . . . On December 8, 1864, this seventeen-year-old soldier died of pneumonia. He is buried in the Confederate Mound at Oak Woods Cemetery, Chicago; a startling revelation unknown to any other living family member.

A discovery of this nature can be both a high and a low point in the search for Confederate ancestors: a high point, in that a forgotten family member is discovered; a low point in the feeling of sadness for all those men, women, and children who were the toll levied by a cruel war. The sacrifice and death of these, our people, deserve to be remembered.

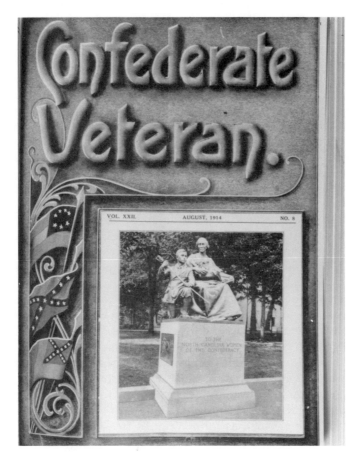

MONUMENT TO THE NORTH CAROLINA WOMEN OF THE CONFEDERACY
From Confederate Veteran Magazine

3

★ NOTABLE SOURCES FOR ★
CONFEDERATE HISTORY

*And ye shall know the truth, and the truth shall
make you free.*

–John 8: 32

*T*HE MATERIAL AVAILABLE FOR STUDY BY A GENEALOGIST
investigating Confederate ancestors is virtually unlimited.
Historians rely basically on printed primary material, such as
original documents, letters, and reports by a reliable contemporary
witness. These firsthand accounts are supplemented by scholarly
secondary sources compiled after the fact. Original historial records
are most valuable to the genealogist, but they should be
supplemented by newspaper stories, obituaries, family letters, oral
tradition, and gravestone inscriptions.

In searching for Confederate ancestors, the genealogist should be
advised to read as much as possible about the era. Although your
ancestor may not be mentioned by name, it is helpful to understand the
battles, sieges, scarcities, and privations that the general population
suffered, in order to understand your ancestor's part in that great
drama.

Any list of recommended historical material is entirely
subjective. As you become more involved in the subject, you will
undoubtedly develop your own list of favorites. Your range of choices
will be great. In the first year after the war, some two thousand books
were published, and the presses have not stopped since. These sources
include regimental, division, and army histories, reminiscences,
autobiographies, sketches, as well as personal narratives of battles,
prison life, and the homefront.

Bibliographies, such as John Wright's two-volume *Compendium
of the Confederacy*; the War Department's *Bibliography of State
Participation in the Civil War*; *Civil War Books: A Critical
Bibliography* by Allan Nevins, James I. Robertson, Jr., and Bell I.
Wiley; and *Travels in the Confederate States: A Bibliography*, a
listing by E. Merton Coulter of 493 titles by soldiers and foreign
observers, will be useful to you when compiling a reading list.

The following recommended reading list is drawn from the
writings of two eminent historians of the period: Douglas Southall
Freeman and Bell Irvin Wiley.

A Southern Woman's Story, by Phoebe Yates Pember, 1879.
[A valuable account of activity in a large Confederate hospital.]

Life of Nathan Bedford Forrest, by John W. A. Wyeth, 1899.
[A well-known biography of the famous cavalry general.]

Destruction and Reconstruction, by Richard Taylor, 1878.
[More forgotten history.]

Heroines of Dixie, by Katherine Jones, 1955.
[Women were highly supportive of the Confederacy, and still are.]

The Land They Fought For, by Clifford Dowdy, 1955.
[One of many outstanding works by this renowned author.]

Civil War and Reconstruction, by James G. Randall, 1953.
[A standard textbook revised by David Donald.]

The Story of the Confederacy, by Robert S. Henry, 1931.
[Among the most outstanding accounts of the Confederate States.]

The Civil War, by Shelby Foote, 1958, 1963, 1974.
[Brilliant narrative trilogy.]

The Rise and Fall of the Confederate Government, by Jefferson Davis, 1881. [Monumental work.]

Constitutional View of the Late War Between the States, by Alexander H. Stephens, 1867. [Strong case is presented.]

The Common Soldier in the Civil War, by Bell I. Wiley, 1958.
[Full text of the author's *Life of Johnny Reb* and *Life of Billy Yank.*]

The Army of Tennessee, by Stanley Horn, 1953.
[The best-known work on this heroic, tragic army, whose soldiers fought with bravery second to none.]

Memoirs of Stonewall Jackson, by Mary Anna Jackson, 1895.

A Diary from Dixie, by Mary Boykin Chesnut, 1905.
[Perhaps the most popular diary of the war.]

A Confederate Girl's Diary, by Sarah Morgan Dawson, 1913.

Recollections Grave and Gay, by Mrs. Burton Harrison, 1911.

Hood's Tennessee Campaign, by Thomas R. Hay, 1929.
["The Gallant Hood of Texas played Hell in Tennessee." None were braver than the men of the Army of Tennessee.]

Christ in the Camp, by J. William Jones, 1888.
[Fine account of religion and revival in Lee's army by one who knew Lee on the battlefield and at home.]

Jeb Stuart, by John W.Thomason, Jr., 1930.
[Mrs. Adele Mitchell, of the Stuart-Mosby Historical Society, says this is the best work on Stuart.]

Military Memoirs of a Confederate, by E. P. Alexander, 1907.
[Penned by the great artillerist of the Army of Northern Virginia.]

The Confederacy, by Albert D. Kirwan, 1959.

Memoirs of the Confederate War for Independence, by Heros von Borcke, 1866. [Written by a Prussian Cavalry officer who served under Jeb Stuart.]

Civil War Prisons, by W. B. Hesseltine, 1930.
[A forgotten study.]

Wearing of the Gray, by John Esten Cooke, 1867.
["Personal Portraits, Scenes, and Adventures of the War" from one who knew Lee's army.]

The South to Posterity, by Douglas S. Freeman, 1939.
[Contains the outstanding bibliography, "The Confederate Bookshelf."]

R. E. Lee, by Douglas S. Freeman, 1934-35.
[Classic 4-volume biography of the military genius.]

Confederate Reminiscences of the Civil War, by John B. Gordon, 1905. [Written by one of Lee's generals, who perhaps is best remembered for his last salute at Appomattox.]

Jefferson Davis . . . A Memoir, by Varina Davis, 1890.

The South Must Have a Rightful Place in History, by Mildred Lewis Rutherford, 1923.

Cracker Culture: Celtic Wars in the Old South, by Grady McWhiney, 1988.

The above list should be viewed as a starting point. Many of these books are available in your library or in reprint editions. Others are hard to find, and rare first editions bring premium prices. Examples of hard-to-find first editions include: *Company "Aytch," Maury Gray's First Tennessee Regiment or a Side Show of the Big Show*, a humorous classic which may be the best ever written by a foot soldier; *Four Years on the Firing Line*, by James Nisbet; *The Trial and Death of Henry Wirz*, an eye-opening account about the commander of theAndersonville prison camp; *A Southern View of the Invasion of the Southern States and War of 1861-1865*, by Capt. Samuel Ashe, the last surviving officer of the Confederate Army; *Giant in Gray*, by Manly W. Wellman, the biography of an unsung hero, Wade Hampton of South Carolina; *Four Years in the Confederate Horse Artillery*, by George Neese; *From Manassas to Appomattox*, by Lt. Gen. James Longstreet; *Behind the Lines of the Southern Confederacy*, by Charles W. Ramsdell; *Story of the Confederate States: Or History of the War for Southern Independence*, by J. T. Derry; *Southern Negroes, 1861-1865*, by Bell I. Wiley; *Southern History of the War*, by Edward A. Pollard; *Dixie After the War*, by Myrta L. Avary; *Rebel Private Front and Rear*, by W. A. Fletcher; *Battles and Leaders of the Civil War*, four volumes edited by Robert U. Johnson and Clarence C. Buel; *One of Jackson's Foot Cavalry*, by John Worsham; *Historic Southern Monuments*, compiled by Mrs. B. A. C. Emerson; *Georgia in the War, 1861-1865*, by Charles E. Jones; *Memoirs of Robert E. Lee*, by A. L. Long; *Sketch of Cobb's Legion of Cavalry*, by Wiley C. Howard; and *Under the Stars and Bars*, by Walter A. Clark. The list could go on and on. Many authoritative works have excellent footnotes and bibliographies, which provide references to other outstanding books.

Genealogists interested in their Confederate ancestors should not stop with the eyewitness accounts or the printed word of historians. They should also explore diaries, original manuscripts, newspapers, magazines, and journals for more information.

CONFEDERATE MONUMENT, EATONTON, GEORGIA, EARLY 20TH CENTURY
Courtesy Georgia Department of Archives and History

WHERE WILL I FIND OUT-OF-PRINT SOURCES FOR CONFEDERATE RESEARCH?

Your state archives has many hard-to-find and out-of-print source materials, as do larger city libraries. Smaller libraries usually do not have extensive Civil War or genealogical collections, but can order books through the inter-library loan system for a nominal fee. Specialty publishing houses, Civil War bookstores, and private dealers sell thousands of items through mail order catalogs. Those who go to flea markets, estate sales, antique shops, and "Civil War" trade shows often find real treasures. Civil War publications contain the names of booksellers in their classifieds and advertisements. The suppliers listed below are by no means the only ones, but they have proven to be reliable, and many mail catalogs to customers:

The Scholar's Bookshelf
110 Melrich Road
Cransbury, NJ 08512

Boonton Bookshop
121 Hawkins Place
Boonton, NJ 07005

Morningside Bookshop
P.O. Box 1087
Dayton, OH 45401

Civil War Books
LSU Press
Baton Rouge, LA 70893

Broadfoot Publishing Co.
Route 4, Box 508-C
Wilmington, NC 28405

Civil War Book Emporium
P.O. Box 157
Huber Heights, OH 45424

The Dixie Press
P.O. Box 110783
Nashville, TN 37222

The Carolina Trader
P.O. Box 769
Monroe, NC 28110

Olde Soldier Books, Inc.
18799 B N. Frederick Rd.
Gaithersburg, MD 20879

All Med. Markt. & Prod., Inc.
4889 Northland Dr., N.E.
Atlanta, GA 30342

Abraham Lincoln Bookshop
357 W. Chicago Ave.
Chicago, IL 60610

Americana Historical Books
Box 1272
Fayetteville, GA 30214

Butternut & Blue
3411 Northwind Road
Baltimore,MD 21234

White Mane Publishing Co.
P.O. Box 152
Shippensburg, PA 17257

CONFEDERATE MANUSCRIPTS, LETTERS, AND DIARIES

Whether written by prominent public figures or common men and women, personal Civil War writings are a valuable research source. These works often reveal feelings that cannot be duplicated by a secondary writer. We should understand that original writings are tangible links to our past, to our heritage, and to American history. It can be an emotional experience to read authentic letters from war-weary wives and soldiers, knowing that our ancestors must have had similar feelings.

Thousands of Confederate manuscripts are available for viewing at locations throughout the South. The University of North Carolina at Chapel Hill and the William R. Perkins Library at Duke University house the largest southern collections in the world. The original Confederate Constitution is in the collection at the University of Georgia. Rare books, maps, and personal papers of famous Confederates are found in libraries, archives, and depositories at the University of Texas, Austin, Emory University, Louisiana State University, the University of South Carolina, Tulane University, the University of Tennessee at Knoxville and Chattanooga, Washington and Lee University, and the University of Virginia. The Departments of Archives and History of all the southern states contain Confederate manuscript collections, either in original, copied, or microfilmed formats. Also, Confederate documents can be found at state institutions, such as the Tennessee State Library and Archives, the White House of the Confederacy in Richmond, and the Museum of the City of Mobile, as well as the Library of Congress—see *A Guide to Collections in the Manuscript Division of the Library of Conqress* (1984), by John R. Sellers—and the National Archives, to name but a few. Check your state or region for such collections. You might discover an ancestral gem, such as in the following reminiscence.

WHITE HOUSE OF THE CONFEDERACY, RICHMOND, VIRGINIA
Courtesy Georgia Department of Archives and History

In this case, the reminiscence was found in a book that was compiled by the UDC, Georgia Division, in the early 1900s. A number of the letters, diaries, and remembrances relates to homelife, faithful servants, battles, soldier's camp life, and the lives of southern women. This particular unpublished note is fascinating, since it involves Gen. Robert E. Lee and a little known incident. It was submitted to the Georgia Department of Archives and History in Atlanta on February 5, 1932, by Mrs. W. T. Leverette of Eatonton, Georgia.

A REMINISCENCE

Of Dr. Nathaniel S. Walker who dressed the only wound of our beloved Gen. R. E. Lee.

Dr. N. S. Walker of Putnam County was a surgeon of the Forty-fourth Georgia Regiment in the army of the Confederacy. He enjoyed the distinction of having been the only surgeon to dress a wound for Robert E. Lee.

General Lee was never hurt by bullet or blade, but the circumstances were these: While returning from the first Maryland campaign, an admiring friend presented a very fine horse to the Confederate commander. The animal, however, was untrained to the bustle of army movements. General Lee was standing, holding the horse, as some artillery wagons rattled by. Frightened, the animal made a sudden plunge, by which the General was thrown violently to the ground and two fingers on his left hand were broken. A soldier from Tennessee, named Cross, was the first to reach his side and give him assistance. Dr. Walker, being near at hand, was called and dressed the wound. He gave General Lee a bottle of linament to relieve the pain. Later in the campaign, they met, and General Lee gave the bottle of linament back to Dr. Walker, telling him to use it to relieve the suffering about them as near as possible, as there was great need of medicine of any kind at that time.

Strange as it may seem, Dr. Walker's son, Dr. Fellow Walker of Milledgeville, met and married Miss Alice Cross of Tennessee, the daughter of the soldier who was first to assist General Lee when the above accident happened.

Fannie Lee Leverette at her writing table,
Eatonton, Georgia, 1911
Courtesy Georgia Department of Archives and History

Dr. Nathaniel Sadler Walker (1830-1902), said to have dressed the only wound
of Gen. Robert E. Lee during the Civil War. *Courtesy Georgia Department of
Archives and History*

EXAMPLE OF A TYPESCRIPT LETTER

The following is an example of a typescript found in the Georgia Department of Archives and History in Atlanta. The original letter was written by Maj. Gilbert J. Wright of Cobb's Legion.

Near Dinwiddie C.H. Va. Oct. 6th 1864

Dear Dorothy,

It has been two or three days since I wrote you. Nothing of importance has transpired, there has been no more fighting. I have been at a private house for two days laid up with my back. I got my boots very wet the day of the fight and at night pulled them off and in pulling them on next morning strained my back. I am able to be about but cannot ride well. I think I shall be well after a day or twos rest. I rec'd a very kind letter from you day before yesterday and was glad to hear that your health was better. I hardly know how to thank you for your kind kind good words to me. If anything gives me more pleasure than anything else it is to know that my wife approves my conduct & sympathizes with me in trouble. Your letters cheer me up and nerves my arm in the contest. I would that our male population possessed one half your patriotism, then Yankee invaders would soon infest our land no longer.

I do not know when I will get a chance to come home as our recent reverses change the aspect of things here. I look for active operations here for at least a full month to come. I would make immediate arrangements for you to come on here but it is very uncertain yet where we will be this winter. I fear there is but little chance for us to come to Georgia this winter to recruit. I will keep you notified as to our movements and prospects; I would ask for leave of absence, but Col King is away sick and I do not know when he will return. My love to Hattie and the balance of the family.

Your Husband

G. J. Wright

CIVIL WAR MAGAZINES, JOURNALS, AND PUBLICATIONS

Today, newsstands are packed with slick photomagazines designed to catch the buyer's eye. Publishers of Civil War magazines have taken note, by adding powerful historic artwork and fresher articles to their offerings. The scholarly journals still rely primarily on the written word, and most of the articles will add spice to the life of a Civil War enthusiast. One word of caution: If an article is to be used as documentation for a research subject, apply the same standards as with other works by checking with other sources to insure reliability.

The following list features quality publications available by subscription, and some which are found on newsstands:

• *America's Civil War* (P.O. Box 383, Mt. Morris, IL 61054-7947) is a glossy magazine loaded with historic art, vintage stills, maps, a "personality" feature, and far-ranging articles.

• *The Confederate Veteran* (P.O. Box 710287, Houston, TX 77271-0287), the official journal of the Sons of Confederate Veterans, is available to non-members. It includes educational features, such as "Attack on the Colors," "Books in Print," and the "South's Last Boys in Gray," as well as historical articles.

• *Blue and Gray* (P.O. Box 28685, Columbus, OH 43228), a magazine "for those who still hear the guns," focuses on battlefield studies and offers travel information for visitation to historic Civil War sites. Outstanding maps, current research, and a preservationist-slant make for interesting reading.

• *The Gettysburg Magazine* (c/o Morningside Bookshop, P.O. Box 1087, Dayton, OH 45401) is a large magazine, billing itself as "historical articles of lasting interest." Ancestral researchers will love the detailed maps and wonderful narratives.

• *Civil War* (P.O. Box 770, Berryville, VA 22611), the magazine of the Civil War Society, includes the Civil War Almanac–a compendium of the news and events for the Civil War enthusiast and a calendar of events by states.

• *Civil War News* (P.O. Box C, 4 RT1, Box 36, Turnbridge, VT 06507), published nine months a year, is a tabloid for Civil War enthusiasts-especially reenactors, preservationists, and historians.

• *The Courier* (2503 Delaware Avenue, Buffalo, NY 14216), a large tabloid newspaper which is loaded with news about reenactments, preservation, collecting, contains numerous advertisements for Civil War items and recruitment for reenactment units.

• *Civil War Regiments* (1475 S. Bascom Avenue, Suite 204, Campbell, CA 95008) is an outstanding new quarterly which features the detailed history of one Union and one Confederate Regiment in each issue. Other features are a preservation report and book review section.

• *Southern Partisan Magazine* (P.O. Box 11708, Columbia, SC 29211). Current southern issues, articles, book reviews.

Scholarly journals include *Civil War History*, published by Kent State University Press, and *The Journal of Confederate History*, edited by Dr. John McGlone, P.O. Box 1615, Murfreesboro, TN 37133. Finally, on the popular front, books like Mike Grissom's *Southern By the Grace of God* and *Last Rebel Yell* (Rebel Press, P.O. Box 158766, Nashville, TN 37215) will prove entertaining.

PHOTOGRAPHS AND VISUAL ART

The War Between the States was the first extensively-photographed war in history. The captured scenes are unforgettable. We may view superbly-mounted troopers awaiting action, poised cannoneers at attention with their beloved artillery, somber generals deep in thought, and panoramic landscapes strewn with wretched corpses longing for decent burial. Civil War art consists of stark photographs by the famed Mathew Brady, beautiful paintings by Gilbert Gaul, Charles Hoffbauer, and Conrad W. Chapman, and bold sketches by common soldiers. All serve as stunning reminders of the way we were. Knowing the names of the subjects is not as important as seeing the impressions and feeling the emotions shown in the faces of these Americans.

Many fine drawings, prints, engravings, and lithographs detail Confederate subjects. Excellent collections are found throughout the country at various locations, such as the Virginia Historical Society, the Museum of the Confederacy in Richmond, and the U.S. Army Military History Institute at Carlisle, Pennsylvania. The Library of Congress holds the most extensive collections of photographs and prints and has contributed to many pictorial books, such as Francis

Miller's, *The Photographic History of the Civil War*; Ezra Warner's, *Generals in Gray*; H. D. Milhollen's, *Embattled Confederates: An Illustrated History of Southerners at War*; and Time-Life Books's, twenty-eight volumes of *The Civil War*. For information on viewing and obtaining copies of historic prints, write the Library of Congress, Washington, D.C. 20540.

This photograph of a shoeless Confederate soldier, a mere boy in death's sleep, conveys the scene in a way that no written word can describe adequately. *Courtesy Library of Congress*

MISCELLANEOUS SOURCES

Researchers often become so fascinated by an ancestor's Confederate military service that they overlook the invaluable contributions of those who served "the cause" in other ways. Men, women, and children of all ages (and many races) toiled in occupations which supported the war effort. They worked as arms makers, cooks, printers, nurses, seamstresses, and spies. Many were employed by the Confederate government and by private firms in the production of saddles, blankets, uniforms, weapons, medicine, and thousands of other items which were necessary to sustain a new nation. Women and loyal blacks assumed the responsibility of operating farms and plantations. Families not only contributed their sons, fathers, and brothers, but also crops from their fields and livestock from their pastures. Documentation of this effort exists in the National Archives microfilm series entitled "Civilian Files," which contains the names of 350,000 individuals and business firms which supplied the Confederacy.

There are many other miscellaneous sources which might yield information on your ancestor. Although Frederick H. Dyer's *Compendium on the War of the Rebellion* deals with Union troops, it also contains a comprehensive listing of every battle fought in each state, which is valuable to any researcher. The 1910 Federal Census indentifies Confederate veterans pardoned for desertion and absence from duty (also found in federal and state amnesty records). One should exercise extreme caution in assuming a soldier was a deserter. Many men served bravely for long periods of time before "leaving" their units to return to their destitute families or defend their home land. Unpublished master's theses written about the Civil War should be consulted. In addition, researchers sometimes overlook the "Captions and Records of Events" cards in the Compiled Service Records, which precede the records of individual soldiers. These cards give summaries of the unit's activities and include information on skirmishes, engagements, and battles which were fought. Also, rich genealogical data can be found in the records of a state's Confederate soldiers' home. The eleven states which comprised the former Confederacy, plus Missouri, Maryland, Kentucky, Oklahoma, and California, had a home for disabled Confederate soldiers. Reminiscences of the old warriors and their wives (who were sometimes residents of the homes) provide great entertainment, even though there are embellishments by aged minds. Less entertaining (and at times tedious) are the official papers of the governor, adjutant general, and quartermaster of the various southern states. Nevertheless, these reports provide useful source material for studying the Confederacy.

The genealogist in search of Confederate ancestors should become familiar with period maps and city directories. These sources are also useful, not only in indentifying the movement of armies and the course of battles, but also in discovering where an ancestor once lived. *A Guide to Civil War Maps of the National Archives* and the *Official Atlas of the Civil War* will pinpoint exact geographic locations and specific battle sites, forts, and cities. Your state, county, or city library might own other maps, which in some cases might reveal the name of property owners in a given area and, as in the case of fire insurance maps, specific houses in each city block. City directories, particularly for 1860, might reveal an ancestor's prewar address and occupation.

MEDALS, DECORATIONS, AND COMMEMORATIVE BADGES

Most Confederate soldiers never received recognition in the form of a medal for their bravery. A withered arm, a game leg, or a glint in the eye when they proclaimed that they had ridden with Forrest or "worn the gray" sufficed for most. The Confederate government intended to issue medals and badges for gallantry, and Congress enacted legislation to that effect, but nothing much became of those efforts, save for the keeping of a partial roll of honor. Medals were authorized by the Confederate Congress, which sometimes voted its thanks to specific commanders or units. Moreover, in a few cases, medals were actually struck, such as those made from Mexican coins for the Confederate victors at Sabine Pass, Texas. But the majority of Confederates were never bestowed medals for their sacrifices.

In an effort to remedy this situation, the United Daughters of the Confederacy, issued southern Crosses of Honor in recognition of the valor and patriotism of the Confederate soldier a generation after the war. The southern Cross of Honor was a prized medal to Confederate veterans (or their descendants in their absence). The design was a cross with a battle flag on the face, surrounded by a wreath of laurel, with the inscription "Deo Vindice 1861-1865." On the obverse side, the inscription read "From the UDC to the UCV: (United Confederate Veterans). By 1913, almost 79,000 medals had been presented. Partial lists of those who received the medal are extant in some UDC records. In later years, the UDC awarded the Cross of Military Service to veterans of other American wars who were lineal descendants of Confederate solders and sailors. In modern times, the Sons of Confederate Veterans has begun to issue posthumous Confederate Medals of Honor to deserving Confederates.

THE SOUTHERN CROSS OF HONOR

OBVERSE   REVERSE

Photographs of the Replica by the Editor

-4-

★ YOUR ANCESTOR'S CONFEDERATE ★
MILITARY UNIT

Steady men, and remember where you are from.
— Gen. M. C. Butler of South Carolina,
during a cavalry charge at Trevillian Station

GEN. M. C. BUTLER
From Confederate Veteran Magazine

*I*N HIS *MEMOIRS OF THE CONFEDERATE WAR OF INDEPENDENCE,*
written in 1866, Maj. Heros von Borcke, a Prussian cavalry officer
serving on Gen. Jeb Stuart's staff, provides insight into the soldier of
the South:

> . . . leaning against a tree, the lifeblood streaming down his side
> from a mortal wound, and his face with the pallor of
> approaching death, 'Major,' said the poor lad, 'I am dying, and

shall never see my regiment again; but I ask you to tell my
comrades that the Yankees have killed but not conquered me.'
Such was the universal spirit of our men, and in this lay the
secret of many of our wonderful accomplishments.

In order to understand this spirit, it is necessary to understand the
organization of the Confederate Army.

Confederate military units were based upon time-honored
southern concepts of kith and kin. A Confederate soldier enlisting in a
local company stood in ranks composed of his brothers, uncles, cousins,
and neighbors, and his unit might even be commanded by his father.
Serving with relatives and neighbors had devastating effect when a
unit suffered high casualties, but it also gave the southern soldier a
psychological edge and a motivation to perform well in front of his
"own people." These local companies were grouped into regiments
from the same general locale (Middle Tennessee, North Mississippi)
and in brigades and divisions from the same or neighboring states.
Southerners fought to the bitter end and often to the death in their
original units. In the last sad days of the war, decimated regiments
were often consolidated into composite units, such as the
1st/6th/8th/9th/27th Tennessee Infantry. Nevertheless, survivors
maintained their pride in the "old" 1st Tennessee, 48th Georgia, or
7th Virginia Regiments.

A review of the Confederate military organization is helpful in
understanding research material found concerning your ancestor's unit.
The following is a brief summary of how units were organized, based
upon historian William Scaife's statistical research.

THE COMPANY

The company was the basic tactical unit, composed of from sixty to one
hundred or more men. Commanded by a captain, this unit often bore
distinguishing nicknames, such as "Volunteers," "Invincibles,"
"Guards," "Riflemen," "Rangers," "Tigers," "Lincoln Killers,"
"Avengers," or "Sharpshooters." The official designation was by an
alphabetic letter: Company A, B, etc. Those units under independent
commands held different designations, but they were generally
identified by their commander's name. The following list identifies
the basic military branches of the Confederate States Army, and the
common divisions within each branch:

• Volunteer Infantry–heavy, light, sharpshooters.

• Artillery–garrison, sea coast, siege, light, horse, organized as "batteries" with one to six guns.

• Cavalry–regular, independent, partisan.

• Legions–a small army composed of artillery, cavalry, and infantry. When a unit was separated from a legion, the designation "legion" often was retained (for example, Cobb's Georgia Legion or Hampton's Legion).

• Specialized units–medical, engineer, miners and sappers, secret service, signal corps, bands, invalid corps, and provost guard.

• State troops–militia, reserves, provost guards, and other units designated for military service within the state or for emergency duty.

• Home guards–similar to state troops, often composed of older men, youth, disabled soldiers, and non-conscripts.

• Regulars–the vast majority of Confederate troops were state units inducted into national service (for example, 1st Virginia, 2nd Georgia, etc.). Yet a few regular (national) units were raised and named 1st Confederate Cavalry, etc.

THE REGIMENT

Commanded by a colonel, regiments (ten companies) averaged from 750 to 1,000 men at the beginning of the war and diminished to 300 or less by 1865. The 1st Tennessee Infantry, for example, left Nashville in May 1861 with 1,200 men, added 2,000 during the war, and surrendered in North Carolina with only 125 in its ranks. A unit was most often given a numerical and state designation, such as the 12th Alabama Volunteer Infantry or the 1st North Carolina Cavalry. Some regiments were named after a person, like the Jeff Davis Legion or Phillips' Georgia Legion. A regiment contained several "battalions," composed of 2 to 9 companies and commanded by a major. Occasionally, battalions served independent of the regiment.

THE BRIGADE

Commanded by a brigadier general, infantry brigades (comprised of four to six regiments) averaged from three to six thousand men and were named after their commanders, such as (George) Maney's Tennessee Brigade and (Claudius) Sears's Mississippi Brigade. If the commander was killed or otherwise removed from command, his name (and that of his replacement) would be used to name the brigade, as in the Doles-Cook Brigade of the Army of Northern Virginia.

THE DIVISION

Commanded by a major general, this force (composed of two or three brigades) was the grand tactical unit that averaged from nine to twelve thousand men. Divisions were also named for their commanders, such as (Jubal A.) Early's Division and (William W.) Loring's Division.

THE ARMY CORPS

Most often commanded by a lieutenant general, infantry corps (comprised of two or three divisions) averaged anywhere from eighteen to thrity thousand soldiers. Famous Confederate Army Corps included Longstreet's and Hardee's. Cavalry Corps, though smaller in number, likewise existed, such as (Joseph) Wheeler's Cavalry.

THE ARMY

Commanded by a full general, such as Robert E. Lee or Joseph E. Johnston, the Army (composed one or more corps) was the major fighting component. Well-known armies of the Confederacy were the Army of Northern Virginia and the Army of Tennessee. There were also lesser known (and smaller) armies, including the Army of the Trans-Mississippi, the Army of the Northwest, and the Army of New Mexico. The largest Confederate armies contained some sixty to ninety thousand men, but in the last year of the war, fifty percent or more of these troops would be lost without replacements. Union forces often numbered over one hundred thousand and could sustain those numbers throughout the conflict. In the majority of battles, Confederate armies were substantially outnumbered.

Confederate armies were usually named for a geographic area (Army of Tennessee), while Union armies were often named for a river (Army of the Potomac, Army of the Ohio, Army of the Cumberland). This rule does not always hold fast, however, particularly early in the war, when the Confederate army in Virginia, under Joseph E. Johnston, was known as the Army of the Potomac, a name later applied to the Union forces fighting in the Eastern Theater under McClellan, Burnside, and Meade, et al.

RESEARCH SOURCES FOR CONFEDERATE MILITARY UNITS

Surprisingly, most Confederate military units never had a formal history, written or published. Information can be located, however, that will allow the researcher to reach a good historical understanding of an ancestor's unit. Available sources provide the following data: when, where, and how the unit was formed; the names of officers; the names of engagements, battles, and campaigns in which the unit participated; casualty figures; and significant dates, including surrender.

Books on individual units vary in quality and quantity. Larger, scholarly books provide excellent detail on battles and often analyze a specific military unit's activity. Magnificent first-person books have been penned by enlisted men with literary talent. Information is available in the form of narratives, personal letters, memoirs, reminiscences, and articles found in libraries and archives. In lieu of finding letters written by your ancestor, firsthand accounts written by members of your ancestor's unit provide the best understanding of his wartime experiences. A number of well-documented regimental histories were published in the late nineteenth and early twentieth centuries. Some modern books contain maps with regiments and brigades detailed by battle positions. Sources run the gamut, from mammoth volumes on famed units, such as the Army of Tennessee, Hood's Texas Brigade, Pelham's Artillery, or the Army of Northern Virginia, to the mere mention of little-known units in archival clippings or well-worn pamphlets.

The quest for information almost never ends. Once you begin your genealogical project, you will discover an insatiable desire to locate one additional tidbit that sheds even more light on the Confederate experience. Tracking your ancestor's military unit is perhaps the greatest challenge and undoubtedly provides the greatest reward in doing Confederate research.

RUTLEDGE'S TENNESSEE BATTERY
Courtesy Tennessee State Library and Archives

WHERE TO BEGIN?

The following sources will serve as a starting point for locating information on Confederate units:

> *Units of the Confederate States Armies,* by Joseph H. Crute, 1987. [*Listing of regiments by states, with brief histories.*]

> *Confederate Military History,* compiled by Gen. Clement A. Evans, 1899 (reprint by Broadfoot Publishing Co., 1987). [*Containing twelve volumes with index, this state-by-state history of Confederate service is one of the earliest and best sources for regimental information. Written in a narrative style, the reference work focuses on units in each southern state. To assist in locating the regiment's state, the following list is offered: Vol. 1-General History; Vol. 2-Maryland & West Va; Vol. 3-Virginia; Vol. 4-North Carolina; Vol. 5-South Carolina; Vol. 6-Georgia; Vol. 7-Alabama & Mississippi; Vol. 8-Tennessee; Vol. 9-Kentucky & Missouri; Vol. 10-Louisiana & Arkansas; Vol. 11-Texas and Louisiana; Vol. 12- General Index.*]

GEN. CLEMENT A. EVANS, PHOTOGRAPHED IN 1913, AT A UCV MEETING
From Confederate Veteran Magazine

Military Bibliography of the Civil War, by C. E. Dornsbusch, 4 volumes (reprint by Morningside Bookshop, 1988).

Southern Historical Society Papers, 52 volumes, with index, 1876, (reprint by Broadfoot Publishing Co., 1990). [*Includes a cross reference chart for Confederate units and their local designation.*]

War of the Rebellion: A Compilation of the Official Records of the Union and Confederate Armies, 128 in 70 volumes, including index, 1881-1901. *The Official Records of the Union and Confederate Navies in the War of the Rebellion*, 31 volumes, including index, 1894-1927. [*Historian Bell I. Wiley calls this series "a monumental work . . . basic to any study of the Civil War." The most basic and useful tool for conducting research on the war. It is often referred to as simply "O.R." (and especially in footnotes as OR).*]

Civil War Books: A Critical Bibliography, compiled by Allan Nevins, James I. Robertson, Jr., and Bell I. Wiley, 2 volumes (reprint by Broadfoot Publishing Co., 1970). [*Widely accepted as the most authoritative guide to Civil War books by renowned authorities.*]

Bibliography of State Participation in the Civil War, U.S. Government Printing Office, 1913. [*Lists works about regiments and other organizations, by state.*]

Confederate Veteran Magazine, 1893-1932, with 3-volume index. [*Many units are mentioned in the 20,000 pages of veterans' accounts, sketches, and reminiscences. Also contains over 4,000 photos, including those of some of the units which held reunions after the war.*]

Officers in the Confederate States Navy, 1861-1865, Naval War Records Office, 1898.

Confederate Military Land Units, by William Tancig, 1967.

List of Field Officers, Regiments, and Battalions in the Confederate Army, 1983.

CONFEDERATE MONUMENT UNVEILING, MONTGOMERY, ALABAMA, 1898
From History of Confederated Southern Memorial Associations

HOW DO I CONDUCT RESEARCH IN THE OFFICIAL RECORDS (O.R.)?

The *O.R.* is of great value to the researcher, and, as you become familiar with the source, you will find it indispensable. The U.S. War Department began publishing this work in 1881. It ultimately provided 138,579 pages of official records, correspondence, orders, returns, and maps for both Confederate and Union forces. Completed in 1901, the *O.R.* has been the most-quoted source of military history by Civil War scholars and authors. The volumes are divided into four series:

Series	# of Volumes	Principal Topics
I	111	Battle reports of all military operations in the field
II	8	Documents relating to prisoners of war and state or politicalprisoners
III	5	Union correspondence, orders, reports, and returns
IV	3	CSA correspondence, orders, reports, and returns

The 128th volume is the General Index, which is a consolidation of all the indexes from each volume. An atlas includes over one thousand maps and sketches.

HOW TO LOCATE A SUBJECT IN THE O.R.

As an example, I will track a favorite subject of mine: Cobb's Legion, a Georgia regiment (my great-great-grandfather's).

Step 1:
Locate the subject in the General Index. To find a military unit, first look under "State" and then "Troops," which will list under the heading several branches, infantry, artillery, cavalry, and miscellaneous. The roman numerals given after the subject provide direction to the particular series volumes, while the arabic numerals indicate the volume in the series. Therefore, the subject, Cobb's Legion, is found under "Georgia, Troops--Miscellaneous."

Step 2:
Locate the subject in the index of the volumes indicated. Again, find "State" and "Troops" in the index of the volume. The numerical notations after the regimental name refer to the pages where the subject is mentioned. In this case, the first volume listed in the General Index is Volume 4. The index in that volume refers the reader to the specified pages. ☞Note: this step should be repeated several times, if there are a number of volumes where the subject is mentioned.

Step 3:
When leafing through the volume, an abundance of correspondence and reports might be encountered. Sometimes the subject is briefly mentioned, while on other occasions much has been written. The researcher will make the decision concerning the value of the information as it relates to the individual research project. Military organizational charts are valuable to unit research of a particular campaign. Note: When I first found my ancestor's organization in the O.R., you could imagine my delight in discovering that his regiment was brigaded under Gen. Wade Hampton, as a part of Gen. J.E.B. Stuart's Cavalry Corps, Army of Northern Virginia. This revelation opened up for me a whole new realm of research subjects, such as Hampton, Stuart, campaigns of the Army of Northern Virginia, as well as the battles of Brandy Station and Gettysburg.

GEORGIA—GERMAN.   349

Georgia Troops (C.)—Continued.
Infantry—Regiments:
17th, I, 5, 11, 12, 19, 21, 27, 29–32, 36, 40, 42, 46, 51; IV, 1, 2.
18th, I, 4–6, 11, 12, 19, 21, 25, 27, 29–32, 36, 42, 43, 46, 51; III, 4 ; IV, 1.
19th, I, 5, 6, 11, 12, 19, 21, 25, 27, 28, 35, 36, 42, 46, 47, 51; IV, 1.
20th, I, 5, 11, 12, 19, 21, 27, 29–32, 36, 40, 42, 46, 51; IV, 1.
21st, I, 5, 11, 12, 19, 21, 25, 27, 29, 33, 36, 42, 43, 46, 51; IV, 1.
22d, I, 4, 11, 12, 19, 21, 25, 27, 29, 33, 36, 42, 46, 51; IV, 1.
23d, I, 4, 9, 11, 19, 21, 25, 27, 28, 35, 36, 42, 46, 47; II, 1; IV, 1.
24th, I, 4, 11, 19, 21, 25, 27, 29–32, 36, 42, 43, 46, 51; IV, 1.
25th, I, 14, 18, 24, 30–32, 38, 39, 45, 47, 53 ; IV, 1.
26th, I, 6, 11+, 12, 14, 19, 21, 25, 27, 29, 36, 42, 43, 46, 51; IV, 1.
27th, I, 5, 11+, 19, 21, 24, 25, 27, 28, 35, 36, 42, 46, 47; IV, 1.
28th, I, 5, 11, 19, 21, 25, 27, 28, 35, 36, 42, 46, 47, 51; IV, 1.
29th, I, 14, 18, 24, 28, 30–32, 35, 38, 39, 45, 47; IV, 1.
30th, I, 14, 18, 24, 28, 30–32, 35, 38, 39, 45, 47, 51, 52.
31st, I, 11, 12, 14, 19, 21, 24, 25, 27, 29, 36, 42, 43, 46, 51, 53.
32d, I, 14, 18, 28, 35+, 38, 42, 44, 47; II, 7.
33d, Littlefield, I, 52.

Georgia Troops (C.)—Continued.
Infantry—Regiments :
57th, I, 16, 20, 24, 28, 30, 32, 35, 38, 39, 45, 47; II, 4, 6, 7.
59th, I, 14, 18, 19, 27–32, 36, 40, 42, 46 ; II, 4.
60th, I, 11, 12, 19, 21, 25, 27, 29, 36, 42, 43, 46, 51.
61st, I, 11, 12, 19, 21, 25, 27, 29, 36, 42, 43, 46, 51.
63d, I, 14, 28, 32, 33, 35, 38, 39, 45, 47.
64th, I, 28, 33, 35, 36, 40, 42, 46, 51 ; IV, 3.
65th, I, 23, 30–32+, 35, 38, 39, 45, 47.
66th, I, 31, 32, 38, 39, 45, 47.
76th (?), I, 46.
Fulton County Militia, I, 38, 52.
Troup County Militia, I, 52.
Miscellaneous :
Cherokee Legion (State), I, 52; IV, 3.
Cobb's Legion, I, 4, 9, 11, 12, 19, 21, 25, 27, 29–33,   ★★★★★★★★
     36, 40, 42, 43, 46, 47, 51; IV, 1, 3.
Dade County Home Guards, I, 32+, 39.
Emanuel County Militia, I, 53.
Floyd Legion (State), I, 52 ; IV, 2, 3.
Moore's Militia, I, 39.
Phillips Legion, I, 5, 6, 11, 12, 14, 19, 21, 25, 27, 29–33, 36, 40, 42, 43, 46, 47, 51, 53 ; IV, 1, 3.
Smith's Legion, I, 16, 20, 23, 53; II, 4.
Washington County Militia, I, 53.
Georgia Troops (U.).
Infantry—Battalions:
1st, I, 49.
Gephart, John, I, 16.
Gerald, Anson R., I, 41.

Step 1: This general index shows that there are twenty volumes from Series I and two from Series IV which contain material on the subject of Cobb's Legion.

Step 2: This specific volume index shows that the unit is mentioned four times.

Artillery.

Maj. WILLIAM T. POAGUE.

Albemarle (Virginia) Artillery, Capt. James W. Wyatt.
Charlotte (North Carolina) Artillery, Capt. Joseph Graham.
Madison (Mississippi) Light Artillery, Capt. George Ward.
Virginia Battery, Capt. J. V. Brooke.

ARTILLERY RESERVE.

Col. R. LINDSAY WALKER.

McIntosh's Battalion.	*Pegram's Battalion.*
Maj. D. G. McINTOSH.	Maj. W. J. PEGRAM. Capt. E. B. BRUNSON.
Danville (Virginia) Artillery, Capt. R. S. Rice. Hardaway (Alabama) Artillery, Capt. W. B. Hurt. 2d Rockbridge (Virginia) Artillery, Lieut. Samuel Wallace. Virginia Battery, Capt. M. Johnson.	Crenshaw (Virginia) Battery. Fredericksburg (Virginia) Artillery, Capt. E. A. Marye. Letcher (Virginia) Artillery, Capt. T. A. Brander. Pee Dee (South Carolina) Artillery, Lieut. William E. Zimmerman. Purcell (Virginia) Artillery, Capt. Joseph McGraw.

CAVALRY.

STUART'S DIVISION.

Maj. Gen. J. E. B. STUART.

Hampton's Brigade.	*Fitz. Lee's Brigade.*
Brig. Gen. WADE HAMPTON. Col. L. S. BAKER.	Brig. Gen. FITZ. LEE.

1st North Carolina, Col. L. S. Baker.
1st South Carolina.
2d South Carolina.
Cobb's (Georgia) Legion.
Jeff. Davis Legion.
Phillips (Georgia) Legion.
	1st Maryland Battalion : †
	    Maj. Harry Gilmor.
	    Maj. Ridgely Brown.
	1st Virginia, Col. James H. Drake.
	2d Virginia, Col. T. T. Munford.
	3d Virginia, Col. Thomas H. Owen.
	4th Virginia, Col. Williams C. Wickham.
	5th Virginia, Col. T. L. Rosser.

Robertson's Brigade.	*Jenkins' Brigade.*
Brig. Gen. BEVERLY H. ROBERTSON.*	Brig. Gen. A. G. JENKINS. Col. M. J. FERGUSON.
4th North Carolina, Col. D. D. Ferebee. 5th North Carolina.	14th Virginia. 16th Virginia. 17th Virginia. 34th Virginia Battalion, Lieut. Col. V. A. Witcher. 36th Virginia Battalion. Jackson's (Virginia) Battery, Capt. Thomas E. Jackson.

****

* Commanded his own and W. E. Jones' brigade.   † Serving with Ewell's corps.

Step 3: Military organizational chart from the *O.R.*

WHAT IF THE O.R. AND OTHER REFERENCE SOURCES ARE NOT AVAILABLE IN NEARBY LIBRARIES?

Aside from traveling to the "holding" facility, there are some research institutions, as well as public and private researchers, who will assist you, especially if the research topic is Confederate military units. For example, The Confederate Research Center (Hill College, 112 Lamar Drive, Hillsboro, Texas 76645) and the U.S. Army Military History Institute (Carlisle Barracks, Building 22, Carlisle, PA 17013-5008) are especially adept at answering inquiries and can provide capsule histories for military units. John F. Walters' Institute for Civil War Research (79-B 67th Drive, Middle Village, NY 11379) offers the research service of locating and copying every page in the *O.R.* that refers to a specific unit. In addition, Walters provides excellent capsule histories of military units at a reasonable charge and information on other Confederate subjects.

In some areas, out-of-print books and even the *O.R.* may be borrowed through inter-library loan. Although "long distance" or "mail" research can be slow and unwieldy, much can still be accomplished.

ONE-ARMED CONFEDERATE VETERAN HARDY SMITH
Courtesy Georgia Department of Archives and History

★ CONDUCTING RESEARCH IN SOUTHERN ★ STATE ARCHIVES AND LIBRARIES

There is much to admire about the Confederacy.
−Shelby Foote

ARCHIVAL COLLECTIONS IN SOUTHERN STATES ARE USUALLY found in the state capital, either as part of a department of history or grouped with the state library or historic commission. Over the decades and centuries, these modern institutions have evolved from private holdings, early historic societies, and warehouses of government records. They have survived fire, flood, war, and neglect. While they contain much valuable information about our ancestors, they are often poorly funded and understaffed. The devoted employees of these organizations are more than willing to assist the novice researcher. Nevertheless, before visiting a repository, you will do well to familiarize yourself with archival and library research.

State archives hold literally tons of records in handwritten, printed, typed, microfilmed, and computer-stored format. Most researchers are interested in items dealing specifically with their own family. But, with help from this book and a friendly staff member, you will be able to locate other sources available in your state archives: land records, maps, reports, legislative proceedings, and many other historical documents which can shed additional light on your Confederate ancestor.

HOW DO I CONDUCT RESEARCH IN THE STATE ARCHIVES?

Many first-time visitors are overwhelmed by the vastness of holdings. Uneasiness comes from inexperience, but this feeling can be overcome quickly! The *secret* to Confederate ancestral research is to focus on those sources which provide pertinent genealogical documentation for an ancestor's participation in the War Between the States.

Instead of floundering, the beginner researcher could begin immediately to find information from sources, such as census records, family exchange files, county histories, will books, land records, genealogy publications, marriage records, and military service microfilm. The researcher should learn how to use a microfilm and microfiche viewer (staff members or other patrons can demonstrate quickly); with practice, you will become adept at its operation. As you learn about sources and their location in the archives, your confidence will soar!

CONFEDERATE SOURCES IN SOUTHERN STATE ARCHIVES

Southern state archives hold a great amount of research material which should be of interest to those performing research on Confederate subjects. Researchers will find manuscripts, Confederate documents, historical publications, and wartime letters of soldiers and their family members. Each of the·southern state archives listed in this section has provided information concerning their Confederate research materials. A great many specific titles are available but not be included in this general listing. Information for state troops might not always be available, but the staff will help you with your research interests. James C. Neagle's *Confederate Research Sources: A Guide to Confederate Archives Collections* and Dr. George Schweitzer's *Civil War Genealogy* are reliable sources.

WHERE IS THE BEST PLACE TO SEARCH FOR INFORMATION ABOUT CONFEDERATE SOLDIERS?

Dr. William D. McCain, Adjutant-in-Chief of the Sons of Confederate Veterans, says: "The best source of information on the service record of a Confederate veteran is the State Department of Archives and History in the state in which he enlisted in the Confederate States Army."

CAN CONFEDERATE SOURCES BE CHECKED BY MAIL?

Archives staff members will generally respond to specific requests, if adequate information is provided in the letter. If detailed research is required, you will be directed to visit the facility or hire a professional genealogist. State archives provide referral lists of recommended genealogists, but you should check references and establish a fee before any work is begun. The Civil War Descendents Society (P.O. Box 233, Athens, Alabama 35611) will research, for a small charge, Federal census records and standard military service records for Confederate soldiers and military units.

CONFEDERATE RESEARCH MATERIALS FOUND IN SOUTHERN STATE ARCHIVES

ALABAMA

State of Alabama
Department of Archives and History
624 Washington Ave.
Montgomery, AL 36130

Archival Services   (205) 242-4152
Reference Room   (205) 242-4435

• Brief history of most Alabama Confederate units
• Muster rolls for most of the companies
• 1907 Census of Confederate veterans living in Alabama
• Pension applications for Civil War veterans and their wives
• Civil War veteran's service index file containing brief information
    on Confederate veterans
• Historical reference file: CSA materials
• Oaths of Allegiance for officers
• Casualties and deaths in hospitals
• Lists of substitutes

ARKANSAS

Arkansas History Commission
One Capitol Mall
Little Rock, AR 72201

General Information (501) 682-6900

• State pension applications

• Ex-Confederate amnesty papers
• Arkansas Confederate Home resident records
• 1911-12 Census of Confederate veterans living in Arkansas
• Confederate military history books
• Registry of Confederate soldiers, sailors, and citizens who died in Federal prisons
• Confederate casualty lists and battle reports by state
• Confederate naval and marine personnel records
• *Records of Louisiana Confederate Soldiers and Louisiana Confederate Commands*, compiled by A. B. Booth, 1920
• *Tennesseans in the Civil War: A Military History of Confederate and Union Units with Available Rosters of Personnel*, 2 parts, 1965
• Index to Confederate pensions of Oklahoma
• Index to Confederate pensions of Tennessee
• Index to Confederate pensions of Texas
• *Confederate Veteran* magazine, 1893-1932
• *Arkansas in the War, 1861-1865*, by Marcus J. Wright, 1963

FLORIDA

Florida State Archives
R. A. Gray Building
Division of Library and Information Services
South Bronough Street
Tallahassee, FL 32399-0250

Archives   (904) 487-2073
Library   (904) 487-2651

• 12,775 approved and denied Confederate pension applications
• Detailed veterans' and widows' pension files
• Comptroller's tax rolls for Florida counties
• Civil War records and history of Florida's State Military Forces are compiled through the Department of Military Affairs files
• Manuscript and genealogical collections
• Soldiers of Florida in the Seminole, Indian, Civil, and Spanish American Wars, by Florida Board of State Institutions, 1909

GEORGIA

Georgia Department of Archives and History
330 Capitol Avenue
Atlanta, GA 30334

General Information   (404) 656-2356
Reference Services   (404) 656-2350

• Civil War records of the governor and the adjutant general
• Muster rolls of Georgia state troops and the Georgia State Line
• Veterans' families supplied with salt, 1862-64
• Rosters of Georgia troops found in the records of Probate Court, formerly the Ordinary's Office
• State pension applications for Confederate veterans and widows
• Alphabetical card file which references Georgians with Confederate Service
• Quartermaster general's files
• Register of Inmates of the Confederate Soldiers' Home of Georgia
• *Roster of the Confederate Soldiers of Georgia, 1861-1865*, compiled by Lillian Henderson, 1955-64. [Contains service records of Georgia's 66 regiments of volunteer infantry.]
• *Georgia in the War, 1861-1865*, by Charles E. Jones, 1909
• UDC typescripts of soldier's letters by military unit

KENTUCKY

Kentucky Public Records Division
Archives Research Room
P.O. Box 537
Frankfort, KY 40602-0537

General Information   (502) 564-3016

Note: The State Archives has National Archives microfilm, but other major sources will be found nearby at the Kentucky Historical Society, Old State Capitol, P.O. Box H, Frankfort, KY, 40602-2108.

• Adjutant General's reports and rosters of Confederate soldiers from Kentucky
• Indexed rosters of Kentucky soldiers serving in Confederate units

- •Index of Confederate pension applications and approved pension files
- •Collection of Kentucky county histories
- • *Report . . . Confederate Kentucky Volunteers,* Kentucky Adjutant General's Office, 1915
- •Published genealogy collections
- •Registration of Confederate and Union veterans' graves
- •Kentucky Confederate Soldiers' Home records
- • Adjutant General's Civil War letters, manuscripts, and special collections

LOUISIANA

Louisiana Secretary of State
Archives and Records Division
P.O. Box 94125
Baton Rouge, LA 70804

General Information   (504) 922-1200

- •Alphabetized list of Louisianians who enlisted in Confederate units, as well as information on the Confederate units
- • *Records of Louisiana Confederate Soldiers and Louisiana Confederate Commands,* compiled by A. B. Booth, 1920
- •Confederate pension applications
- • *Military Record of Louisiana, Biographical and Historical Papers Relating to the Military Organization of the State,* by Napier Bartlett, Adjutant
- •Records of the Adjutant General, 1850-65
- • The Rebel Archives-official papers from the Office of the Adjutant General, 1855-63

MISSISSIPPI

Mississippi Department of Archives & History
100 South State Street
P.O. Box 571
Jackson, MS 39205

General Information   (601) 359-6876

• Index to Mississippi Confederate soldiers
• Mississippi pension applications and records
• Military unit histories
• Official Confederate military records include more than 100,000 cards containing the name, rank, and organization of Mississippi soldiers
• Some original muster rolls
• Manuscript collections
• Military service discharges, 1862-64
• Register of commissions, Army of Mississippi, 1861-65
• Deceased Confederate soldiers' claims
• Requisitions for supplies

NORTH CAROLINA

North Carolina Department of Archives and History
109 East Jones Street
Raleigh, NC 27611

General Information   (919) 733-3952

• Confederate pension applications and records
• *North Carolina Troops, 1861-1865, A Roster*, compiled by Louis H. Manarin, 1966-
• State Adjutant General's Roll of Honor
• Enlistment bounty payrolls
• Roster of the Militia officers of North Carolina, 1862-65
• Confederate Soldier's Home roll and register, 1890-1917
• UDC Confederate burial place survey
• *Guide to Civil War Records in the North Carolina State Archives* and *A Guide to Military Organizations and Installations, North Carolina, 1861-1865*
• Alphabetically arranged abstracts on cards of John W. Moore's *Roster of North Carolina Troops in the War Between the States*

SOUTH CAROLINA

South Carolina Department of Archives and History
P.O. Box 11669
Capitol Station

Columbia, SC 29211

General Information   (803) 734-8577

- •Combined alphabetical index of Confederate soldiers
- •Adjutant General and State Confederate Historian's rolls of volunteers (5 volumes)
- •Confederate Historian's Roll of Honor and Roll of deceased South Carolina troops
- •Pension applications and records, 1919-25
- •Artificial limb applications, 1879-99
- •Confederate Infirmary (Home) applications, 1909-39
- •Confederate Home applications of wives, widows, sisters, and daughters, 1909-57
- •South Carolina Troops in Confederate Service, compiled by Alexander S. Salley, 1913-14, 1930
- •Legislative check stubs record Confederate soldiers who were transported to Gettysburg

TENNESSEE

Tennessee State Library and Archives
403 7th Avenue, North
Nashville, TN 37243-0312

General Information   (615) 741-2764

- •*Tennesseans in the Civil War: A Military History of Confederate and Union Units with Available Rosters of Personnel*, 2 parts, 1965
- •Confederate pension applications and records
- •*Tennessee Civil War Veterans Questionnaires*, 5 volumes, 1985
  [*Questionnaires are from 1915 to 1922*]
- •Regimental histories of various Tennessee units
- •*Tennessee in the War, 1861-1865* and *Lists of Military Organizations and Officers from Tennessee in both the Confederate and Union Armies*, by Marcus J. Wright, 1908
- •Civil War microfilm catalog
- •Special collections: casualty lists, diaries, letters, order books, etc.
- •Confederate Soldiers' Home records
- •Adjutant General's records, 1861-65

TEXAS

Texas State Library and Archives
Archives Division
P.O. Box 12927
Austin, TX 78711

Archives information   (512) 463-5455

•Civil War records
•Confederate pension applications and records
•Widow's Confederate pension applications
•Ranger units, 1836-1935
•Confederate Home For Men records
•Indigent family lists- An 1863 Act to support families and dependents of Texas soldiers
•Audited military claims of Texas State troops of Civil War era
•Muster roll abstracts for Civil War units
•Biographical index
•*Texas Batteries, Battalions, Regiments, Commanders, and Field Officers, Confederate States Army, 1861-1865*, by Lester L. Fitzhugh, 1959
•*Texas in the War, 1861-1865*, Wright and Simpson, 1965
•Graves of Civil War veterans: Raymond W. Watkins collection

VIRGINIA

Virginia State Library
Archives Division
11th Street at Capitol Square
Richmond, VA 23219

General Information   (804) 786-2306

•Manuscripts (or photocopies of documents) attesting to the military service of some Virginians during the Civil War
•Confederate pension records for veterans, widows, and unmarried or widowed daughters
•Confederate military service records of units and individuals
•The Virginia Regimental Histories Series, 22 volumes-to-date

- *A Guide to Virginia Military Organizations, 1861-1865*, by Lee A. Wallace, Jr., 1964
- Records for men killed in battle
- Prisoner of War records
- Special collections: manuscripts,letters, biographical studies
- Records of the R. E. Lee Confederate Soldiers' Home

OTHER DEPOSITORIES WITH CONFEDERATE RECORDS

Maryland State Archives
Hall of Records
350 Rowe Boulevard
Annapolis, MD 21401

West Virginia
Archives and History Library
Division of Culture and History
The Cultural Center
Charleston, WV 25305

Arkansas History Commission
300 W. Markam Street
Little Rock, AR 72201

Missouri State Library
308 East High Street
Jefferson City, MO 65102

Oklahoma Historical Society
Historical Building
2100 N. Lincoln Blvd.
Oklahoma City, OK 73105

Pennsylvania Historical Society
and Museum
Commission/Archives Bldg.
Box 1076
Harrisburg, PA 17108

Confederate Research Center
Hill Junior College
P.O. Box 619
Hillsboro, TX 78701

State of Missouri
Adjutant General's Office
1717 Industrial Drive
Jefferson City, MO 65101

Louisiana State Museum
751 Chartres Street
New Orleans, LA 70116

Oklahoma State Library
109 State Capitol
Oklahoma City, OK 73105

New Mexico
State Records Center & Archives
404 Montezuma Street
Santa Fe, NM 87501

Delaware Division of Historical
and Cultural Affairs
Hall of Records
Dover, DE 19901

U.S. Army Military History
Institute
Carlisle Barracks, Bldg. 22
Carlisle, PA 17013-5008

THE GREAT SEAL OF THE CONFEDERACY

DEO VINDICE (GOD OUR VINDICATOR)
Courtesy The Museum of the Confederacy

After the Seven Days' Battles, Federal troops burned Col. W. H. F. ("Rooney")
Lee's home in Virginia. This famous, old White House on the Pamunkey had
been the place where George Washington once courted young Martha Curtis.
Southerners vehemently condemned "the deceitfulness of the enemy's pretended
reverence for everything asscociated with the name of Washington." Ironically,
the Confederacy revered Virginian George Washington as the father of their
country, portraying his likeness in the Great Seal of the Confederacy and on
stamp issues.

-6-

★ BEYOND THE DISCOVERY ★
OF CONFEDERATE ANCESTORS

Maybe the disaster, humiliation and suffering of
the South have been our touch by grace. Maybe
we have found redemption in a way we might not
have if we had got what we prayed for. . . . In this
sense, we won the War.
                                    –Edward C. Raffetto
                                    Chaplain-in- Chief
                                    Sons of Confederate Veterans

As YOU COMPLETE YOUR SEARCH AND IDENTIFICATION OF Confederate ancestors, you will discover there are many "kindred spirits," who, like you, wish to expand their genealogical search and become students of the period. For those looking beyond the discovery of Confederate ancestors, there are many avenues to explore, including visiting battlefields, joining historical societies and patriotic organizations of descendants, participating in living history reenactments, going to "Civil War" shows, or delving into the vast literature of the period. As you focus on your interest, you will probably learn that much has been written about the war, and others are interested, too! There are nationwide organizations of descendants of Confederate veterans (such as the United Daughters of the Confederacy, the Sons of Confederate Veterans, and the Children of the Confederacy), organizations which focus on particular battles (like the Franklin Memorial Association), and specialized societies or groups which are interested in particular units (for example, Morgan's Men Association). Whatever your interest, there is probably a group, society, battlefield, or library where you can pursue it. Americans' fascination with that period of history never ends.

Periodically, our national attention is focused on remembrances of *the* War. In the early part of the twentieth century, Union and Confederate veterans still gathered for grand reunions. On the seventy-fifth anniversary of the battle of Gettysburg, the old graybeards gathered at that historic site. When ancient Confederates reenacted Pickett's charge with feint rebel yells, a roar of approval went up from the Union lines, as blueclad veterans surged out to meet their former enemies, embrace them, and wipe the tears from their eyes. Americans still remembered.

Old Warriors Meeting for a Last Reunion at Gettysburg in 1938, the 75th Anniversary of the Battle. *Photo Courtesy Library of Congress*

In the early days of the century, Confederate and Union Memorial days were celebrated with great fanfare and pageantry. Monuments were unveiled before large patriotic audiences, and the longevity of local veterans was celebrated in the press. In more modern times, *Gone With the Wind*, by Margaret Mitchell, became an international bestseller, and the movie focused worldwide attention on the Hollywood version of the Old South. The 1960s' Civil War Centennial refocused public attention on the period, as did the 1980s' 125th-anniversary celebration. Various television shows, movies, and "documentaries" also contributed to rekindling interest in the war. Ken Burns's television miniseries, *The Civil War*, attracted a record number of viewers. Unfortunately, Mr. Burns's simplistic presentation that slavery was *the* cause of the war made the series rather one-sided. Late night talk show hosts and uninformed journalists acclaimed it, but few southern historians found it of lasting value. It was good entertainment but poor history. One positive result, however, was that public attention was again drawn to the period, and many individuals were compelled to seek the truth through more reliable sources.

The opportunities for learning about the period and about Confederate history are numerous. Whether your attention is first captured by a movie, novel, or television series, you will soon learn that the *real* thing is far more interesting!

BATTLEFIELDS

Ancestral research is enhanced by visits to battlefields, historic sites, and cemeteries. Your specific interests will dictate what is most important. There are a number of good travel directories available. One of the best and most comprehensive is Alice Cromie's, *Tour of the Civil War*, which offers a complete state-by-state listing of battlegrounds, landmarks, museums, and sites to visit. Another excellent guide is the Conservation Fund's *Civil War Battlefield Guide*, edited by Frances H. Kennedy, which contains maps and photographs of the highest quality.

National parks and battlefields offer an interesting supplement to genealogical and historic research. After hearing about an ancestor's service or studying a particular battle, you will be thrilled to walk the fields where your ancestor fought and perhaps died. One of the most exciting plans by the Park Service (in conjunction with the National Archives and several national genealogical groups) is to computerize a listing of over 3.5 million Confederate and Union soldiers. This would allow visitors to access information to determine if an ancestor or his regiment were present at a particular battleground! The following is a list of National Park Service Historic Sites associated with the war:

• Abraham Lincoln Birthplace
  National Historic Site
  2995 Lincoln Farm Road
  Hodgenville, KY 42748

• Andersonville National
  Historic Site
  Route 1, Box 85
  Andersonville, GA 31711

• Andrew Johnson National
  Historic Site
  P.O. Box 1088
  Greeneville, TN 37743

• Antietam National Battle-
  field Site and Cemetery
  P.O. Box 158
  Sharpsburg, MD 21782

• Appomattox Court House
  National Historic Park
  P.O. Box 218
  Appomattox, VA 24522

• Arlington House (Lee's Home)
  c/o George Washington
  Memorial Parkway
  Turkey Run Park
  McLean, VA 22101

• Brices Cross Roads National
  Battlefield Site
  c/o Supt., Natchez Trace Parkway
  RR1, NT-143
  Tupelo, MS 38801

• Chickamauga and Chattanooga
  National Military Park
  P.O. Box 2128
  Fort Oglethorpe, GA 30742

• Fort Donelson National Battlefield
  P.O. Box 434
  Dover, TN 37058-0434

• Lincoln Home National
  Historic Site
  413 South Eighth Street
  Springfield, IL 62701

• Lincoln Boyhood National
  Memorial
  Lincoln City, IN 47552

• Stones River National
  Battlefield & Cemetery
  3501 Old Nashville Highway
  Murfreesboro, TN 37129

• Lincoln Memorial
  c/o National Capital Parks, Central
  900 Ohio Drive, S.W.
  Washington, DC 20242

• Manassas National Battle
  field Park
  6511 Sudley Road
  Manassas, VA 22110

• Fort Jefferson National
  Monument
  c/o Everglades National Park
  P.O. Box 279
  Homestead, FL 33030

• Fort Pulaski National
  Monument
  P.O. Box 30757
  Savannah, GA 31410

• Fredericksburg & Spotsylvania
  County Battlefields Memorial
  National Military Park
  and Cemetery
  120 Chatham Lane
  Fredericksburg, VA 22405

• Gen. Grant National Memorial
  122nd St. and Riverside Drive
  New York, NY 10027

- Gettysburg National Military
  Park and Cemetery
  Gettysburg, PA 17325

- Harpers Ferry National
  Historical Park
  P.O. Box 65
  Harpers Ferry, WV 25425

- Kennesaw Mountain National
  Battlefield Park
  P.O. Box 1167
  Marietta, GA 30061

- Monocacy National Battlefield
  P.O. Box 158
  Sharpsburg, MD 21782

- Shiloh National Military
  Park and Cemetery
  P.O. Box 61
  Shiloh, TN 38376

- Tupelo National Battlefield
  c/o Supt., Natchez Trace Parkway
  RR1, NT-143
  Tupelo, MS 38801

- Pea Ridge National
  Military Park
  Pea Ridge, AR 72751

- Richmond National Battlefield Park
  3215 East Broad Street
  Richmond, VA 23223

- Vicksburg National Military
  Park & Cemetery
  3201 Clay Street
  Vicksburg, MS 39180

- Wilson's Creek National
  Battlefield
  Route 2, Box 75
  Republic, MO 65738

Monocacy Battlefield, in Frederick, Maryland, has become the newest park. Other sites associated with the war or Confederate history are under state jurisdiction or in private hands. Many of these sites can be located, and they are designated by historic markers.

CONFEDERATE MEMORIAL, PATRIOTIC, AND HISTORIC ORGANIZATIONS

A great many Confederate memorial and patriotic associations have flourished in the South and across America. Some of these groups fulfilled their original purpose and have become dormant; others are continuing to operate successfully. Through the years, perhaps the most zealous guardians of the memory of the "Lost Cause," aside from the old veterans themselves, have been the women of the South. They have kept the the war years alive for many generations. In more recent times, various organizations have been formed to study the Civil War. These groups and some of the old-line associations are important because they help preserve and foster American history. As Mrs. Leora A. Lawson of the Southern Memorial Associations put it in 1904:

> Our record is, that (Confederate) Memorial Day (April 26) has been made the occasion to pay homage to the memory of our Confederate dead, and our children taught that Southern soldiers were not rebels, but patriots, who in the words of our own General John B. Gordon, 'Fought the bravest fight in the world against the greatest odds.'

THE SONS OF CONFEDERATE VETERANS

Within months following the cessation of hostilities between the North and South in 1865, groups of veterans who had served in the Confederate Army and Navy began organizing throughout the South. Their main objective was the welfare and comfort of the men who had "worn the gray." In time, the veterans' groups realized that their efforts would be more effective if they combined their efforts into one organization. Thus, on June 10, 1889, the United Confederate Veterans was established in New Orleans, Louisiana. On July 1, 1896, during an annual meeting of the United Confederate Veterans in Richmond, Virginia twenty-four "camps," as they were called, from five southern states approved the formation of the "United Sons of Confederate Veterans," with J. E. B. Stuart, Jr., becoming its first leader. In 1912, the name of the organization was shortened to "Sons of Confederate Veterans."

Today the SCV is growing not only in the South but also throughout the nation. It is a voluntary organization of both direct and collateral descendants of those who served honorably in the Confederate Army or Navy. It is patriotic, historical, educational, benevolent, non-political, and non-sectarian. Moreover, the SCV condemns the inappropriate use of Confederate symbols by individuals or groups which espouse political extremism or racial superiority. For membership information, contact the SCV's General Headquarters, P.O. Box 59, Columbia, TN 38401-0059.

Daniel (captured), John (wounded), and Pleasant (died of disease) Chitwood, Co. A, 23rd Georgia Infantry, "Bartow Yankee Killers"

THE UNITED DAUGHTERS OF THE CONFEDERACY

Organized on September 10, 1894, the UDC is the outgrowth of many local memorial, monument and Confederate Home Associations which were organized after the War between the States. It is a non-profit, non-political organization.

The objectives of the organization are: HISTORICAL, EDUCA-TIONAL, BENEVOLENT, MEMORIAL AND PATRIOTIC - to honor the memory of those who served and those who fell in the service of the Confederate States; to protect, preserve, and mark the places made historic by Confederate valor; to collect and preserve the material for a truthful history of the War Between the States; to record the part taken by Southern women in patient endurance of hardship and patriotic devotion during the struggle, as in untiring efforts after the war during the reconstruction of the South; to fulfill the sacred duty of benevolence towards the survivors and towards those dependent upon them; to assist descendants of worthy Confederates in securing proper educa-tion and to cherish the ties of friendship among the members of the Organization.

Those eligible for Active membership are women no less than sixteen years of age who are blood descendants, lineal or collateral, of men and women who served honorably in the Army, Navy, or Civil Service of the Confederate States of America, or gave Material Aid to the Cause. Also eligible are those women who are lineal descendants of members or former members of the UDC.

Proof of eligibility may be obtained from one of the following sources:

- UDC Business Office: From records of military service
  compiled from registered applications and veterans' files.
  (If available)
- State Department of Archives and History:
  Confederate Records
- General Services Administrations, National Archives and
  Records Authoritative Publications

Admission to the Organization is by invitation through a Chapter. For more information, write UDC Business Office, 328 North Boulevard, Richmond, VA 23220-4057. (Please enclosed a stamped self-addressed envelope)

Submitted by:
Mrs. Anthony J. LaCavera, Sr.
President-General
United Daughters of the Confederacy

EMBLEM AND MOTTO OF THE CONFEDERATED
SOUTHERN MEMORIAL ASSOCIATION OF THE SOUTH

CIVIL WAR ROUND TABLES

Since 1940, when the first group formed at Chicago, Civil War Round Tables have promoted distinguished scholarship through 150 chapters around the world. Illustrious Civil War historians, such as Douglas Southall Freeman, Allan Nevins, and Bruce Catton, have been associated with this organization. The Civil War Round Table Associates sponsor national conferences to include the Congress of Civil War Round Tables, the Confederate Historical Institute, the West Coast Civil War Conference, and the Society of Civil War Historians conference. The locally-autonomous chapters welcome those who are interested in the Civil War. For more information, write the Civil War Round Table Associates, P.O. Box 7388, Little Rock, AR 72217.

THE CONFEDERATE MEMORIAL ASSOCIATION

This organization is dedicated to the preservation of southern culture as a part of the American heritage and sponsors the Confederate Memorial Hall (also known as the Confederate Embassy), a national historic landmark in Washington, D.C., which currently houses a museum and library of note. The Confederate Memorial Hall, located just eight blocks from the White House, offers an Old South setting for embassy balls, receptions, and special events. For information, write The Confederate Memorial Hall, 1322 Vermont Avenue, N.W., Washington, D. C. 20005.

Representative of the noble and patriotic women of the South is Miss Ellen Louise Axson, best known as the wife of President Woodrow Wilson. *From Confederate Veteran Magazine*

THE SOUTHERN HISTORICAL ASSOCIATION

Since its founding in 1934, the SHA has promoted research in southern history and presently encourages the teaching and study of all areas of history in the South. In addition to publishing the prestigious *Journal of Southern History*, the association encourages the establishment of state and local historical societies, the preservation of the South's historical records, and its members' attendance at annual meetings. Inquiries concerning membership should be addressed to the Southern Historical Association, University of Georgia, Department of History, Athens, GA 30602.

FRANKLIN MEMORIAL ASSOCIATION

Founded by Ronald T. Clemmons, this organization has succeeded in raising funds to commission busts of the six Confederate generals killed at the Battle of Franklin, and it continues its work (with the able assistance of Tim Burgess) by marking the graves of other Franklin casualties. A newsletter is available by writing the association at P.O. Box 1641, Murfreesboro, TN 37133.

SOCIETY OF CIVIL WAR HISTORIANS

This group was founded by Jerry Russell of Little Rock, Arkansas (Heritagepac, P.O. Box 7388, Little Rock, AR 72217), and its annual meetings are held in conjunction with the SHA. Dr. Anne Bailey, who edits the society's newsletter (which contains book reviews), may be contacted at the Department of History, University of Arkansas, Fayetteville, AR 72701.

HISTORICAL ASSOCIATIONS

Historical societies champion preservation causes and appeal to those who have mutual interests in history. Some distinguished groups with Civil War and Confederate ties are: the Stuart-Mosby Historical Society (215 Garland Drive, Carlisle, PA 17013); the Civil War Society (P.O. Box 770, Berryville, VA 22611); the Confederate Historical Institute (P.O. Box 7388, Little Rock, AR 72217); Hood's Texas Brigade Association (P.O. Box 619, Hillsboro, TX 76645); Robert E. Lee Memorial Association (Stratford Hall Plantation, Stratford, VA 22558); Sam Davis Memorial Association (P.O. Box 1, Smyrna, TN 37167); Jefferson Davis Association (P.O. Box 1892, Rice University, Houston, TX 77251); and the National Society of Andersonville (P.O. Box 65, Andersonville, GA 31711). The Military Order of the Stars and Bars, an adjunct association of the SCV, is for those whose ancestors served in the Confederate officer corps. And the Children of the Confederacy, an adjunct association of the UDC, is for children whose ancestors were in the Confederate military.

Increasing numbers of Civil War reenactment groups are forming. Reenactors are essentially amateur historians who enjoy recreating living history demonstrations and battle scenes. Entire families often participate in reenactments. Information may be obtained from historical societies, SCV camps, and from publications, such as *Camp Chase Gazette* (P.O. Box 707C, Marietta, OH 45750), and *The Civil War News* (Route 1, Box 36, Tunbridge, VT 05077).

CIVIL WAR COLLECTIBLES

Many people (including antique dealers, professional collectors, and hobbyists) are interested in locating Civil War–and especially Confederate–collectibles. The list of items sought seems endless: Civil War books, weapons, swords, currency, bonds, ammunition, jewelry, uniforms, ladies apparel, fine china, buttons, medical instruments, photographs, veterans' memorabilia, figurines, stamps, original documents, letters, and dug relics of every description. Civil War magazines and specialty publications contain advertisements of suppliers. Civil War trade shows, held around the country, draw thousands of dealers. Catalogs and price lists are available from various companies, such as Olde Soldier Books (18779 B North Frederick Avenue, Gaithersburg, MD 20879), and The North South Trader's Civil War (P.O. Box Drawer 631, Orange, VA 22960) provides a magazine for collectors and relic hunters.

Historic Civil War art prints are also becoming very popular as collectibles. These colorful prints are produced in limited quantities (usually under 1,200) and feature poignant historical and battle scenes. Confederate subjects are very popular. The value of the limited edition prints increases every year, often selling on the secondary market for several times the original purchase price. Fine galleries, such as Allen's Creations Frame and Art Gallery (Box 452, Clemson, SC 19633), carry these prints, and will send newsletters and price lists to interested customers. Many of the popular artists–Don Troiani, Rick Reeves, Mort Kunstler, Dale Gallon, Don Stivers, among others–advertise in Civil War magazines.

HISTORIC PRESERVATION

Many Civil War battlefields and historic sites have been "lost" to development. Little remains today of the great battles at Battery

Wagner, Knoxville, Franklin, Atlanta, Chantilly, Seven Pines, and many other locations. Today, historic sites are imperiled by those who have no regard for their nation's history. All Americans should be concerned! The National Park Service is attempting to protect our valuable historic lands, but it is overwhelmed with demands and its budget is strained. In fact, only a miniscule portion of our tax dollars goes to the National Park Service or historic land acquisition and protection. We should consider assisting in historic preservation efforts. Several organizations are working to preserve our historic lands: The Association for the Preservation of Civil War Sites, Inc. (P.O. Box 1862, Fredericksburg, VA 22404); the Civil War Battlefield Campaign of the Conservation Fund (1800 N. Kent Street, Arlington, VA 22209); HERITAGEPAC (Box 7281, Little Rock, AR 72217); Friends of the National Parks at Gettysburg, Inc. (P.O. Box 4622, Gettysburg, PA 17325); and the National Parks and Conservation Association (1776 Massachusetts Avenue, N.W., Washington, D.C. 20077-6404).

MONUMENT IN FORT MILL, SOUTH CAROLINA, TO FAITHFUL SLAVES
From Confederate Veteran Magazine

BLACKS IN CONFEDERATE SERVICE

"Uncle" Jerry Perkins served as a manservant to Charles Perkins, a Confederate enlisted soldier of the 31st Tennessee Infantry. On July 22, 1864, when Charles was killed near Atlanta, Uncle Jerry removed the body from the field and gently buried it in a makeshift box. Later, after walking home to Brownsville, Tennessee, to report the bad news to Charles' family, Uncle Jerry returned with a farm wagon and a metallic coffin to bring his master home.

Southern Literature and tradition are replete such tales of faithful salves who accompanied their masters to war and risked their lives to bring home the body of a fallen young hero. It is not generally known, however, that many slaves and free blacks actually served in combat roles in the Confederate army. It is well-documented that blacks served the Confederacy as teamsters, cooks, bakers, and musicians. Since the difference between the "front lines" and the "rearguard" in a Civil War battle may have been only a few hundred years, these service troops invariably became involved in battle to one extent or another. In addition, many were regularly attached to Confederate units. A U.S. Sanitary Commission observer noted that, when Lee's army passed through Frederick, Maryland, on the way to Sharpsburg, up to ten percent of the Confederate forces under arms were blacks. If this figure is accurate for all Confederate armies, then the proportion of blacks who served with the Confederacy was essentially the same as that with Union forces. The concept of blacks serving the South in a military role shatters many popular conceptions of the causes and effects of the war itself. For example, if Southerners had been primarily fighting to preserve slavery, as some have argued, then they would not have considered emancipation in exchange for European recognition, nor would they have assented to the raising of black Confederate regiments during the final months of the war. Rather, the Confederacy was fighting in defense of hearth and home, as well as for its perception of states' right. Moreover, many southern blacks joined white southerners in resisting northern aggression, not only on the homefront, by producing supplies for the armies, but also in actual battle, for reasons of loyalty and in an effort to prove their worth. They, too, were Confederates.

Much work remains to be done on the role of southern blacks in the Confederate army. Two scholars, Professor Edward Smith of Washington, D.C., and Dr. Richard Rollins of California, have studied this topic for a number of years, and they will contribute a book on the subject to be published later this year by Southern

Heritage Press. Some other notable works which might be useful in tracing black Confederates include: *Southern Negroes, 1861-1865,* by Bell I. Wiley; *Black Writers and the American Civil War,* edited by Richard A. Long (1988); *Black Genealogy,* by Charles L. Blockson and Ron Fry (1977); *Black Genesis,* by James Rose and Alice Eicholz (1978); *Ethnic Genealogy: A Research Guide,* by Jessie C. Smith (1983); and H. C. Blackerby's *Blacks in Blue and Gray* (1979).

Black Confederates at a veterans' gathering. Note the reunion badges and medals. *From Confederate Veteran Magazine*

OTHER GENEALOGICAL RESEARCH

Successfully tracing your family lineage to 1860 might be just the beginning to a new hobby. Amateur genealogists enjoy tracing their ancestry through colonial America and even to the Old World. Numerous genealogical societies (organized in local, regional, or state areas) offer instruction, guidance, and educational programs to those interested in the field. Society meetings feature "how-to" lectures and informative talks on such subjects as "American Indians," "Substitutes for Lost Census Records," and "Scottish Research." Most societies offer low membership fees, quarterly newsletters, and research assistance. Fellowship with the other members is also a great bonus. For information on societies, contact your state archives or write the Federation of Genealogical Societies, P.O. Box 3385, Salt Lake City. Also, you might want to invest in and to explore some of the following helpful genealogical source materials:

Books on Genealogy

•*Unpuzzling Your Past, A Guide to Genealogy,* by Emily Anne Croom, 1989

•*Tracing Your Ancestry,* by F. Wilbur Helmbold, 1977

•*Guide to Genealogical Study in the Archives of the Confederate States of America,* National Archives, 1986

•*A Handy Book for Genealogists,* by George B. Everton, 1991

•*The Source: A Guidebook of American Genealogy Ancestry,* by Arlene Eakle and Joni Cerny, 1984

•*The Genealogist's Address Book,* Genealogical Publishing Co., 1992

•*Genealogical Research--Methods and Sources,* by Milton Rubincam, 1980

Publishers & Suppliers of Genealogical Materials

•Dixie Press, P.O. Box 110783, Nashville, TN 37222

•Ancestry Publishing, P.O. Box 476, Salt Lake City, UT 84110

•The Everton Publishers, Inc., Box 368, Logan, UT 84321

•Genealogical Publishing Company, Inc., 1001 North Calvert Street, Baltimore, MD 21202-3897

•Heritage Books, Inc., 1540-E Pointer Ridge Place, Suite 190, Bowie, MD 20716

•Scholarly Resources, 104 Greenhill Avenue, Wilmington, DE 19805-1897

•National Archives Trust Fund (Genealogical Research Materials), NEPS 735, P.O. Box 100793, Atlanta, GA 30384

•National Genealogical Society, 4527 17th St. North, Arlington, VA 22207

Periodicals on Genealogy

• *Southern Genealogist's Exchange Quarterly*, P.O. Box 2801, Jacksonville, FL 32203

• *National Genealogical Society Quarterly*, 4527 17th Street North, Arlington, VA 22207-2399

• *Prologue: The Journal of the National Archives*, Washington, DC 20036

• *Everson's Genealogical Helper*, Box 368, Logan, UT 84321

SOUTHERN STUDIES AT THE UNIVERSITY LEVEL

Mark Twain once said, "The very ink which all history is written is merely fluid prejudice." The great author was very familiar with the fate of Confederate history, having briefly served with Missouri Confederate State Troops. Today, southern studies are gaining in popularity and "students of the War" are actively learning through self-education and formalized study. The University of Mississippi has established the Center for the Study of Southern Culture, offering degrees in the field. Professors Charles Reagan Wilson and William Ferris have produced the *Encyclopedia of Southern Culture* from this center. Other universities are producing studies and developing programs as well. For example, Marshall University in Huntington, West Virginia, now offers a $5,000 graduate scholarship for Confederate research and writing.

OTHER RESEARCH SITES OF NOTE

The Confederate Research Center of Hill College, P.O. Box 616, Hillsboro, Texas 76645, houses a large number of research sources, especially for Confederate military units. The Museum and White House of the Confederacy, 1201 East Clay Street, Richmond, Virginia 23219, contains the largest Confederate artifact collection in the nation, including displays of the "Great Seal of the Confederacy," Gen. Robert E. Lee's sword and uniform, and Jeb Stuart's plumed hat. An extensive collection of wartime objects and manuscripts may be viewed, and visitors can tour the impeccably-restored last home of

President Jefferson Davis at Biloxi, Mississippi (Beauvoir, 2244 Beach Blvd., Biloxi, MS 39581). The Confederate Museum of New Orleans (929 Camp Street, New Olreans, LA 70130), established in 1891, contains uniforms, weapons, flags, as well as personal effects of Confederate leaders.

Good luck with your Confederate genealogical search, wherever it might lead you. Remember, if you locate information or have experiences not mentioned in this volume, please notify the Author, J. H. Segars (c/o Historical Research, P.O. Box 347163, Atlanta, GA 30334) for possible inclusion in future editions.

Gen. Robert E. Lee: the epitome of all that is good and noble in the South.

–John McGlone
Lee's Birthday Toast, 1993
Greenville, South Carolina

★ EPILOGUE ★

The Civil War is the crux of our history. You cannot understand any part of our past, from the convening of the Constitutional Convention down to this morning without eventually arriving at the Civil War.

    –Bernard De Voto

AMERICANS ARE STILL IN DISAGREEMENT OVER THE CAUSES AND effects of our greatest national experience–the War Between the States. From the outset, southerners were acutely aware that history would be written by the victors, and that omissions and revisions would be the rule. Even Gen. Robert E. Lee felt compelled to make a statement concerning Confederate history. "The reputation of individuals is of minor importance," he said, compared "to the opinion posterity may form of the motives which govern the people of the South in their late struggle for the maintenance of the principles of the Constitution. I hope, therefore, a true history will be written, and justice done them." Today, revisionists are asking us to accept Civil War history in a simplistic manner. Political activists want Confederate symbols removed, while others go so far as to suggest that southerners forget their history altogether. In a world of "political correctness," how can we learn the truth about the war itself and our ancestors' part in it?

Historians and genealogists understand where the answers are. They are not buried with dead forebears, but live in the historic documents and papers which have survived. The challenge for the Confederate ancestral researcher is to locate these documents and retrieve the information contained therein. In this manner, from tracing our Confederate ancestry, we can come face to face with history and perhaps find the answers to our questions.

The first southerner invited to address the renowned New England Society in New York City was Henry W. Grady, a Georgia journalist and scholar. As a boy, Grady had seen the drastic effects of war in his home state, and he had personally suffered the loss of a Confederate soldier-father at Petersburg. On December 21, 1886, Grady's oration, "The New South," received world-wide acclaim and brought instant fame to the speaker. His oration was interpreted then, and generally regarded now, as a catalyst for great sectional healing for both the North and South.

In this day and age, the words of Henry Grady are, unfortunately, largely forgotten. He spoke not only with eloquence but also with a profound authority possessed by one who had lived in both the Old and New South. Grady knew the minds of our ancestors. Although his oratory was cheered wildly by most Americans then, Grady would not be as popular today. "This is said in no spirit of timeserving or apology," Grady explained.

> The South has nothing for which to apologize. She believes that the late struggle between the states was war and not rebellion, revolution and not conspiracy, and that her convictions were as honest as yours. I should be unjust to the dauntless spirit of the South and to my own convictions if I did not make this plain in this presence. The South has nothing to take back.

It should be noted that there are many today who strongly agree with these immortal words of Henry Grady, as well as with those of earlier generations who have venerated their Confederate heritage. While traveling in the West during the early 1900s, the venerable Grand Historian of the UDC, Mildred Lewis Rutherford, was approached by a fellow sojourner, a rather opiniated gentleman, who spoke to the point. "Miss Rutherford," he declared, "my father was a Confederate soldier; but had he lived, I am sure he would have regretted having fought on the wrong side!" Cool and deliberate, the aristocratic woman replied: "Far more probably, he would have regretted having a son so disloyal to the principles for which he was willing to give his life." As surely as this man misunderstood and undervalued his father's patriotism to the Confederacy, oftentimes so do we.

For those willing to search for the men and women of the old Confederacy, the journey will prove to be challenging, fascinating, and, above all, enlightening. The conclusions drawn from the search will be unpredictable, and they are best interpreted by the individual researcher. Nevertheless, one conclusion is apparent: the heroic efforts of all Americans should not be forgotten.

How should we as Confederate descendants react to our own history? Perhaps the answer was best stated in 1901 by a Confederate daughter, Mrs. Mattie Bruce Reynolds of Kentucky, who admonished southerners to:

> Instill in the minds, first of all, of our children and grandchildren, the courage and devotion of their ancestors in the path of what was duty—not bitterness, nothing incompatible with the love of the Union—then they must know the true history of the war.

In discovering our Confederate ancestors, we honor the legacy of a truly brave and intrepid host. That legacy enriches the American heritage and demonstrates that our nation's greatness is derived not only from the diversity of a people who are alive today but also from those who have labored valiantly in the past.

Spring 1996   J. H. Segars
                                                    Lawrenceville, Ga.

MONUMENT TO UNKNOWN CONFEDERATE DEAD
OAKLAND CEMETERY, ATLANTA, GEORGIA

I asked God for strength, that I
might achieve,

I was made weak, that I might
learn humbly to obey.

I asked for health, that I might
do greater things,

I was given infirmity, that I might
do better things.

I asked for riches, that I might be happy,

I was given poverty, that I might be wise.

I asked for power, that I might have
the praise of men,

I was given weakness, that I
might feel the need of God.

I asked for all things, that I
might enjoy life,

I was given life, that I might
enjoy all things.

I got nothing that I ask for—
but everything I had hoped for.

Almost despite myself, my
unspoken prayers were answered.

I am, among all men,
most richly blessed.

–Anonymous Confederate Soldier

BIBLIOGRAPHIC NOTE

All titles appearing in this volume constitute a full bibliography as recommended by the author. See especially pages 45-47, 66-67, and 99-100.

Titles not previously mentioned:

Annie Heloise Abel, *The American Indian in the Civil War, 1865-1865*, 1992
Cecil Chesterton, *A History of the United States*, 1919
Mary A. H. Gay, *Life in Dixie During the War*, 1901
Ron Gragg, *The Illustrated Confederate Reader*, 1989
William R. Scaife, *The Campaign for Atlanta*, 1985
George K. Schweitzer, *Civil War Genealogy*, 1988
Twelve Southerners, *I'll Take My Stand*, 1930

ACKNOWLEDGMENTS

One of life's pleasures comes from encountering those unique spiritual souls who, like Grady, love their heritage and understand the important things in life: people who have a passion for the past, a curiosity about the present, and a vision for the future. Among those of this order who have greatly contibuted to this book are: E. J. Hardigree, Jim and Kathy Teasley, Montgomery Hudson, Katherine Walters, Linda Adams, Dr. Glenn Pethel, Dr. John McGlone, and Dr. R. B. Rosenburg.

A number of organizations have provided information and counsel: notably, various state archives throughout the South; the Confederate Research Center of Hill College, Texas; the Georgia Genealogical Society; The United Daughters of the Confederacy; The Sons of Confederate Veterans; and a host of historical associations. Two staff members at the Georgia Department of Archives and History in Atlanta, Charlotte Ray, Civil War Research Advisor, and Gail Miller, Photo Archivist, particularly made significant contributions, as did Hazel Purdie, county bibliographer and staff librarian with the Georgia Department of Education for some forty-six years. Special appreciation is also extended to my wife, Marie Hitchcock Segars, whose ancestors served with Gen. James Longstreet, and to my children, Scott and Paige. May they dare to live life as courageously as their southern forebears. And may we all be steadfast in the faith of our ancestors as taught in John 14: 6.

THE AUTHOR

J. H. Segars serves as an administrator with the Georgia Department of Education in Atlanta. A native of Eatonton, Georgia, he earned a B. A. degree from the State University of West Georgia. His ancestors served in Cobb's Georgia Legion, Wade Hampton's Brigade, Stuart's Cavalry Corps, ANV. Segars is the editor of *Andersonville: The Southern Perspective* and *Forgotten Confederates: An Anthology about Black Southerners.*

THE EDITOR

John McGlone, a graduate of Georgetown University, received a doctorate in history with an emphasis on historic preservation. Dr. McGlone teaches college courses and is the founder and editor in chief of the *Journal of Confederate History*. His Confederate ancestors (to include General J. O. Shelby) served in the Army of Tennessee and the Trans-Mississippi West.

INDEX

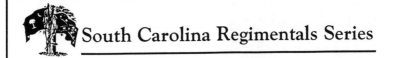

South Carolina Regimentals Series

MEMOIRS OF THE WAR OF SECESSION by Johnson Hagood, BG, CSA. Orig. Pub. 1909. Reprinted 1989. 496 pp. Illustrated and Indexed, Acid Free Paper, Hard Cover. $32.00
Describes the history and service of "Hagood's Brigade," and the battles and skirmishes of the 11th, 21st, 25th and 27th Regiments and the 7th (Rion's) Battalion in Virginia, North Carolina and South Carolina. Also organization and roster of the 1st South Carolina Volunteers (Hagood's).

BUTLER AND HIS CAVALRY: 1861-1865 by U.R.Brooks. Orig. Pub. 1911. Reprinted 1990. 594 pp. Illustrated and Indexed, Acid Free Paper, Hard Cover.$32.00
History and stories of the 4th, 5th and 6th South Carolina Cavalry Regiments, which would later become "Butler's Brigade." Also an account of Butler's rise from captain in the Hampton Legion to major general of the division. Of particular interest are the cavalry actions of the '64 Virginia Campaign and the '65 Carolinas Campaign.

STORIES OF THE CONFEDERACY by U. R. Brooks. Orig. Pub. Reprinted 1991. 410 pp. Illustrated and Indexed, Acid Free Paper, Hard Cover.$32.00
U. R. Brooks joined the Confederate cavalry in 1862 at age 16. His service took him first to the Carolina coast, then to Virginia where he participated in some of the most bitter cavalry fighting of the war. Following the war he was an active force in the survivors and veterans organizations, in which capacity he became the unofficial historian of his peers.

REMINISCENCES OF A PRIVATE by Frank M. Mixson. Orig. Pub. 1910. Reprinted 1990. 135 pp. Acid Free Paper, Hard Cover.$22.00
Beginning his service around Charleston, Mixson proceeded with his unit--Co E, 1st SCV, Jenkins' Brigade--to Virginia where he participated in all his regiment's engagements. Excellent coverage of the East Tennessee Campaign, Spottsylvania and the attempt to recover Fort Harrison in September '64.
Douglas Southall Freeman said this book was, "One of the best and frankest narratives of a private soldier..."

A SKETCH OF THE WAR RECORD OF THE EDISTO RIFLES: 1861-1865 by William Valmore Izlar. Orig. Pub. 1914. Reprinted 1991. 216pp. Acid Free Paper, Hard Cover. $24.00
The story of an ornamental antebellum militia company's transformation into a hardened wartime regiment. The Edisto Rifles were a militia company from South Carolina's Orangeburg District that volunteered for Confederate service after the attack on Fort Sumter. In the army reorganization of '62 they became the Eutaw Regiment of the 25th South Carolina Volunteers. They saw action at Petersburg, James Island, Secessionville, Battery Wagner, Fort Fisher, Town Creek, Kinston and Bentonville.

CAPTAIN ALEXANDER HAMILTON BOYKIN: ONE OF SOUTH CAROLINA'S DISTINGUISHED CITIZENS by Richard Manning Boykin. Orig. Pub. 1942. Reprinted 1991. 170pp. Acid Free Paper, Hard Cover. $20.00
Written by the subject's grandson, this book is the memoir of the life of a planter-soldier from South Carolina's Kershaw District. A. H. Boykin raised and equipped 'Boykin's Rangers,' a cavalry company which accompanied J. E. B. Stuart on his famous 'ride round McClellan.' Also gives an account of Boykin's recovery and restoration of his property after the War.

THE FALLING FLAG by Edward M. Boykin. Orig. Pub. 1874. Reprinted 1991. Acid Free Paper, Hard Cover. September delivery date.$28.00
Story of the final days of Lee's army from the Richmond withdrawal to Appomattox. Written by the commander of the 7th South Carolina cavalry.

Ordering Information: Enclose check plus $3.00 shipping and handling to Jim Fox, 9 Precipice Rd, Camden South Carolina 29029

Journal of Confederate History
KH-Paperbacks

Southern Books

IN SEARCH OF CONFEDERATE ANCESTORS; THE GUIDE by J. H. Segars. An acclaimed "how-to" guide for both the beginning genealogist and the more experienced family researcher. Now in the fourth printing; 45 photos, illustration, charts, 112 pages. $10 soft cover.

ONE OF THE MOST DARING OF MEN: THE LIFE OF CONFEDERATE GENERAL WILLIAM TATUM WOFFORD by Gerald J. Smith. The first full length biography of General Wofford, one of Robert E. Lee's unsung commanders. The Georgians under Wofford's command served with distinction alongside the men of Hood's Texas Brigade. This life and times of this General have been overlooked by everyone except the author, a professor of history and Georgia historian. Photos, maps, index, bibliography, 255 pages, $15 soft cover.

FORGOTTEN CONFEDERATES; AN ANTHOLOGY ABOUT BLACK SOUTHERNERS who served in Confederate armies. This extraordinary books, edited by Barrow, Segars, and Rosenburg, examines the role of African Americans who served within Southern armies. Includes source material by Confederate veterans, excerpts from official records, 34 photographs and illustrations, 193 pages; $15 for soft cover, $21 for hardback with dust jacket.

VALOR AND LACE: THE ROLES OF CONFEDERATE WOMEN 1861-1865 edited by Mauiel Joslyn. This book examines the various roles of Confederate Women and includes chapter about women who were POW's, soldiers, defenders, and angels of mercy. Photographs, footnotes; 200 pages; $15 soft cover.

ANDERSONVILLE: THE SOUTHERN PERSPECTIVE edited by J. H. Segars. Finally, the true story of Confederate Camp Sumter as seen through the eyes of Southerners past and present. Includes articles by William R. Scaife, Mauriel Joslyn, Edwin C. Bearss, Heinrich Wirz, Edward A. Pollard, Mildred Rutherford. 46 photos, maps, illustrations; 191 pages; $15 soft cover.

TO ORDER, send check or money order (plus $1.50 per book shipping) to Southern Lion Books, Post Office Box 347163, Atlanta, GA 30334.

Southern Lion Books is a publisher and wholesaler of fine books about the South. We specialize in Civil War reprints and in producing books about southern cultures. Southern Lion Books is proud to offer reprints of the *Journal of Confederate History* Book Series and inquires from dealers and general readers are welcome.

THE COURIER
Civil War
Newspaper

- Do you collect, buy, sell, or trade Civil War memorabilia?

- Are you searching for specific information relating to a certain battle, prison, ship, regiment, or individual who fought in the Civil War?

- Do you provide goods/services for Civil War buffs?

- Are you recruiting members for a CWRT, SCV, SUV, Reenactment or Skirmish organization, or similar group of buffs?

IF SO, **THE COURIER** WILL HELP YOU!
SEND FOR A **FREE** SAMPLE COPY TODAY!
(Please allow up to 4-5 weeks for delivery)

— — — — — — — — — — — — — - clip here - — — — — — — — — — — — — — —

Yes, I'd like to receive a free copy of **THE COURIER**.
Please send it to: *(Please print)*

NAME: _____

ADDRESS: _____

CITY: _____

STATE: _____ ZIP: _____

THE COURIER
2503 Delaware Ave. • Buffalo, New York 14216
Phone (716) 873-2594 • FAX (716) 873-0809

PLEASE CHECK ONE:

_____ Reenactor

_____ Skirmisher

_____ SUV

_____ SCV

_____ CWRT

_____ Other